★ WHY ★

BERNIE SANDERS

★ MATTERS ★

D0029428

★ WHY ★

BERNIE SANDERS

★ MATTERS ★

HARRY JAFFE

Regan Arts.

NEW YORK

Regan Arts.

65 Bleecker Street
New York, NY 10012

First Regan Arts paperback edition, December 2015.

Library of Congress Control Number: 2015958508

ISBN 978-1-68245-017-8

Interior design by Nancy Singer
Cover design by Catherine Casalino

Printed in the United States of America

10 9 8 7 6 5 4 3 2 1

To Louise, who never doubted me.
In memory of Bobby Weinberg, who would have
gotten a huge kick out of Bernie for President.

CONTENTS

"POWER TO THE PEOPLE"

In the early evening of September 22, 2015, I was biking across the busy intersection of Seventh Street and Massachusetts Avenue Northwest, in downtown Washington, DC, when I saw Senator Bernard Sanders and his wife, Jane, engaged in conversation with a tall African American man astride a bicycle. The biker was pleading with Sanders about the need for job training in the city. "I'll vote for you to be president," he said, "but I need a job."

Sanders listened, then waved him off and crossed Seventh Street.

I couldn't believe my luck. For months I had been trying to land an interview with the candidate for the Democratic nomination. He'd ignored my pleas and brushed me off the one time I ambushed him in the Senate office building. And here he was, fresh from greeting Pope Francis at the White House. Fair game, I figured.

"Senator," I said, "are you ever going to let me interview you? I'm working on your biography."

He turned and scowled. "Hey, I'm trying to take a walk with my wife," he growled.

"But, but—"

He hailed a cab, hustled inside with Jane, and headed down Massachusetts Avenue toward Union Station. I stood there and wondered: *Did that just happen?*

Unfortunately it did. I would never get that interview with Sanders. In his quarter century on Capitol Hill, in the House of Representatives and the Senate, he has rarely granted an interview about his life beyond politics and policy.

When Simon Van Zuylen-Wood, writing for the *National Journal*, asked Sanders why he chose to spend his early adult life living hand-to-mouth after growing up economically insecure, the senator snapped, "You're my psychoanalyst here? What?"

For Sanders, allowing a journalist to delve into his past to understand his motivation, his character, the genesis of his political positions is a waste of time. He has no interest in revealing himself. Most politicians running for president have written autobiographies that try to give voters a glimpse into their past, albeit a very rosy one. Barack Obama wrote two. Sanders wrote a book in 1997, but it's largely about his political life.

Bernie Sanders is a uniquely American political success story. He grew up in a lower middle-class home in a Jewish neighborhood in Brooklyn, became a radical in college, and then took the edge off his radicalism to get elected in Vermont as mayor, congressman, and senator. Defying political analysts and odds makers, he rode a wave of economic discontent and mounted a strong campaign to be president in 2016. The seventy-four-year-old New York Jew came off as the authentic visionary of the American dream, appealing to eighteen-year-old college students, farmers, factory workers, and retirees.

What is the source of Sanders's appeal? What are the source's origins? Where and how did he develop his principles on workers and wealth? How did he become a socialist? What did that mean to him then—and now? How did he practice socialism in his early days? How did he develop his ability to excite crowds? How can he make an audience forget that he talks like a deli guy and sometimes looks like a rumpled old man ranting about rich people?

Sanders would rather you didn't know.

Why Bernie Sanders Matters is the first unauthorized biography of the senator who wants to be president. With a cadre of researchers, I have spent months delving into Sanders's past, talking to friends, allies, enemies, and, finally, his wife. Now I can describe the genesis of his political theories: how he constructed his philosophy brick by brick, how he stumbled into the role of politician, how he built the "Bernie!" brand. He was always ambitious, always looking for the next political rung, always confounding his enemies and exceeding expectations.

"Never underestimate Bernard," says John Franco, a

xii   ★ WHY BERNIE SANDERS MATTERS ★

member of his ad hoc Vermont inner circle. "It's a mistake that many have made."

Why Bernie Sanders Matters is a tale of:

* Flatbush, where he wanted to be an athlete; learned about Jewish shtetl life; got a taste of working-class, left-leaning Jews amid communists and "red-diaper babies"; and he attended James Madison High School, whose alumni include Ruth Bader Ginsburg and Senator Chuck Schumer.
* The University of Chicago, where he first learned and practiced radical politics.
* An Israeli kibbutz, where he saw socialism at work and encountered the rural, communal life that drew him to Vermont.
* Vermont in the 1970s, a unique political petri dish and perhaps the only place in America where he could have thrived and risen to power.
* Washington, DC, where, despite his monomaniacal adherence to working-class economic issues and his dyspeptic approach to collegiality, he achieved quite a bit, especially for America's veterans.

The two words that best describe Sanders's personal and political history are "surprise" and "shock." He has often surprised himself and shocked his political rivals. For example, he has thrived on being the underdog no one takes seriously. He first started talking about the gap between rich and poor in America and the disappearing middle class in 1970, forty-five years before he announced his White House bid. He was considered an anomaly and ignored. Most politicians would have changed course at that point, added to their core message, broadened their scope. Not Sanders. Every speech, every appearance he hammered away on the economic and political forces that were killing America's middle class. He did it when it was out of fashion, when Republican conservatives scoffed at him, and when the Democrats dismissed him. Now income inequality and saving the middle class are the economic issues of the day.

That's only one of the reasons Bernie Sanders matters.

★ WHY ★

BERNIE SANDERS

★ MATTERS ★

ONE

THE EVANGELIST

"There are a lotta people here.
A lotta. I cannot believe this crowd."
—BERNIE SANDERS, Phoenix, July 18, 2015

The Penn Branch Shopping Center sits at the top of Pennsylvania Avenue as it crests a hill overlooking Washington, DC, from the east. On a clear day, when the leaves are off the trees, you can glimpse the tops of landmarks in the nation's capital city: the US Capitol dome, the Washington Monument, the Jefferson Memorial.

This stretch of Pennsylvania Avenue bears little resemblance to the power corridor between the White House and the Capitol, the grand boulevard that some call "America's Main Street" because it hosts the Inaugural Parade every four years. Penn Branch occupies a corner of the other Washington, the one that stretches along the part of Pennsylvania

Avenue that runs east of the Anacostia River, where middle-
and lower-class African American families struggle to make
it in neighborhoods just a few miles from the nation's halls of
power. The shopping center is a row of fifteen shabby storefronts strung along a cramped parking lot. The windows of
the beauty salon are cracked. The restaurant-supply store has
gone out of business. You have to drive miles to find a sit-
down restaurant. But the liquor store and check-cashing joint
are bustling. Unemployment in surrounding neighborhoods is
around 15 percent; black youth unemployment hovers around
50 percent.

Penn Branch, where small businesses go to die, is the setting for Raymond Bell's lifelong dream. Up a dusty staircase
and down a long, narrow hall Bell runs the HOPE Project out
of a corner office on the strip mall's second floor. For nearly a
decade the nonprofit, which stands for Helping Other People
Excel, has offered free classes to train low-income, predominantly African American young adults for information-
technology jobs. In a job-training field that's not known for
positive outcomes, Bell can point to a roster of success stories. His program has trained 375 students since 2010, most
of whom have found well-paying jobs in the region's burgeoning government-contracting sector. Brandon Craig enrolled in
HOPE while working at a Virginia liquor store, completed the
course, and landed jobs with Hewlett-Packard and then a US
Navy contractor. Sonya Davis went from credit union teller to
analyst for the Commerce Department. Alyssia Suarez graduated from the program in 2012 and signed on with a defense
contractor in Herndon, Virginia.

"These young people are energetic, smart, and talented,"

says the tall, wiry, bespectacled Bell. "All they need is strict, straightforward training."

On June 4, 2015, a red Ford Focus with Vermont plates pulled up to the door leading to the HOPE offices. US Senator Bernard Sanders swung his long legs out the back door and pulled himself up. He reached back in for a yellow legal pad and tried to organize the sheets of paper sticking out of it. He looked around and scowled, as if he had arrived at a wake. "Is this it?" he asked.

A week earlier, before a rousing crowd in Burlington, his political base, the seventy-three-year-old Vermont senator had officially launched his campaign for president. The audience thrilled to his call to arms for the "political revolution" he would commandeer from the White House. He embraced his "brothuhs and sistuhs" as if the thousands who came to listen were among his political intimates. Many were. But Sanders returned to a nation's capital that was unimpressed. The visit to HOPE had been on his schedule for weeks, yet no news cameras, no hordes of reporters, no rope lines to hold back fans greeted his arrival. If Hillary Rodham Clinton, his principal competition for the Democratic nomination, had shown up, reporters would have been elbowing each other aside for a better glimpse of the former secretary of state.

Sanders, though, was unfazed. He had come to HOPE to unveil the Employ Young Americans Now Bill, his latest legislation to stem high unemployment. It would allot $5.5 billion in federal aid to states to employ young people in summer and year-round jobs. He entered the program's cramped rooms to find more than a dozen students sitting at rows of tables with desktop computers. The only cameras were from a couple of local TV stations. Sanders smiled and waved as he walked to the lectern and microphone at the front of the class beneath a sign on the wall that read "Harvard of the 'Hood."

"In America now we spend nearly $200 billion on public safety, including $70 billion on correctional facilities, each and every year," Sanders told the students and the sprinkling of reporters. He loves to pepper his rhetoric with numbers and data. "So let me be very clear: in my view it makes a lot more sense to invest in jobs, in job training, and in education than spending incredible amounts of money on jails and law enforcement."

He mentioned unemployment five times, prison twice, jobs a dozen. He called the fact that one in three black males will spend time in prison "an unspeakable tragedy" and described the rate of youth unemployment as an "international disgrace." He never uttered the words "White House," "president," or "campaign."

Congressman John Conyers from Detroit, who had arrived late, seconded Sanders's point, praised him for his devotion to job training in tough neighborhoods, and excused himself. Sanders congratulated the students and disappeared into a small conference room, where he talked for about twenty minutes with Bell and a few graduates, including the program's "superstar" alumna, Phyllis Ussery, who now earned $60,000 a year at an IT job. Sanders then quietly slipped back to the red compact car. Aides drove him down the hill and across the Anacostia River to the other Pennsylvania Avenue, where a different, less hopeful reality awaited his job-training bill.

Covering the event for *Bloomberg Politics*, David Weigel wrote that a $5.5 billion social program would have had a rough road even in a Democratic Congress: "In a Capitol controlled by Republicans, it might as well propose taxing churches to pay for sex-reassignment surgeries on a moon base."

Sanders was well aware of the odds against his bill, but the political reality didn't seem to matter. In keeping with his crusade to remake America in his image, he had recently renewed legislative efforts to raise $1 trillion to fix the nation's infrastructure and $750 billion in new taxes on overseas profits to fund free tuition for all students at state colleges and universities. A few weeks later he introduced legislation to increase estate taxes for anyone inheriting more than $3.5 million, with a top rate of 50 percent for those inheriting $10 million to $50 million. At the same time he was working on legislation to raise the minimum wage to $15 an hour.

None of Sanders's proposals would see its way out of congressional committees; few would get a hearing; and none would become law. But that didn't seem to deter Vermont's junior senator, before or after he became a presidential candidate. He had been a man on a mission since he arrived in Congress almost a quarter-century earlier. In his calculus, proposals stacked up in the bins of unpassed bills were building blocks for the foundation of the Bernie Sanders movement. As much as he was a politician, Sanders was an educator. More than that, he was a proselytizer.

★ ★ ★

Sanders didn't play the role of a freshly minted presidential candidate. Nor did he have the aura of a US senator, one of one hundred statesmen in the most powerful upper chamber on the planet. As always he was the unsmiling man in a gray rumpled suit, rushing through his day. There was so much to be done if he was going to save the nation from the scourge of greedy billionaires.

From the day he came to Washington as a congressman-elect in 1990, Sanders set himself apart. Congress was a club he refused to join. He treated the institution like enemy turf: Bernie in the Lion's Den with 434 legislators who were part of a suspect system. He arrived unaffiliated, the first Independent in Congress in forty years. For most of the next twenty-five years—sixteen in the House and nine in the Senate—he preferred to operate on his own, as if he were a solo legislator. He compiled a record as the most left-leaning member in all of Congress at the time. Underscoring his loner status, in his 1997 book, *Outsider in the House*, he described a debate on raising the minimum wage this way: "Same old lies. Same old bullshit. Same old empty sound-and-fury."

He occasionally took baby steps toward the mainstream. For instance, in the House he founded the Congressional Progressive Caucus, and in the Senate he successfully amended many bills and chaired the Veterans Affairs Committee with skill, if not camaraderie. But Sanders was most comfortable in the role of rebel, irritant, subversive. Since 1971, through his entire political life and twenty campaigns, he has raged against the machine.

"I am not afraid to call myself a radical," he told a gathering of supporters and reporters after winning his third mayoral race in Burlington in 1986.

"I am a socialist, and everyone knows that," he said upon his election to Congress in 1990.

Asked by the *Nation* in July 2015 if he minded critics calling him a socialist, he said, "Do they think I'm afraid of the word? I'm not afraid of the word."

★ ★ ★

Hillary Rodham Clinton didn't seem worried when Sanders stood on the lawn of the Capitol in April 2015 and announced his intention to run for president. "I welcome him into the race," she tweeted. At that point the former secretary of state had little to fear. She was the clear leader of the small pack of Democrats seeking the nomination. She had been building a juggernaut staff and raising millions of dollars in contributions for more than a year. Former Baltimore mayor Martin O'Malley hoped to mount a challenge as the young, fresh-faced, next-generation Democratic leader. Former senator Jim Webb came with a pre-presidential résumé; a decorated marine during the Vietnam War, Webb had served as secretary of the navy before becoming Virginia's junior senator in 2007. Lincoln Chafee, who had run for office from Rhode Island as both a Republican and a Democrat, also entered the race. Clinton seemed vulnerable to a challenge from the left, and many Democrats clamored for Senator Elizabeth Warren from Massachusetts to step into the race. She declined.

The slate of GOP candidates in the spring of 2015 was too voluminous to keep track of. At one point the number of hopefuls reached seventeen. To the surprise and consternation of the Republican political establishment, billionaire developer and TV reality show star Donald Trump was running neck and neck with Ben Carson, a retired surgeon and the darling of social conservatives who wanted to ban all abortions and roll back a host of social programs, including Medicare and Medicaid.

The campaigning was roiling and rambunctious through the summer of 2015. You cannot tell what will happen in politics. Ever. And you must never discount the element of surprise.

★ ★ ★

Sanders seemed genuinely surprised, shocked even, when he mounted the podium and gazed out at the huge crowd that had come to hear him speak at New Hampshire's Nashua Community College on June 27, 2015, a little more than three weeks after his visit to HOPE. They stood and clapped and whooped and hollered as if they were about to hear Mick Jagger and the Rolling Stones.

Sanders's eyes got wide behind his thick glasses. He raised his hands to quiet the crowd and even seemed to crack a smile. He thanked the woman who had introduced him. He didn't welcome or thank the crowd or lighten it up with a joke. He just set sail.

"When we began we were considered fringe, out of touch, not serious," he said slowly and deliberately, "but I think that has been changing in New Hampshire, Iowa, and around the country in the last couple of weeks."

After starting in single digits, Sanders's poll numbers had begun to rise; contributions were flowing into his campaign; and volunteers were signing up. "The reason I think we are doing well is that we are running a different type of campaign," he continued in his quiet, professorial voice. "This is a campaign being run by and involving millions of ordinary Americans. Right now we have many hundreds of thousands of people who have signed onto this campaign in every state in this country."

The crowd roared, eager to join the momentum. And Sanders was only minutes into an hour-long speech.

When Sanders had pulled up around 10:30 that morning in a Ford Fiesta and climbed out of the backseat clutching his yellow pad, the Nashua Community College gym floor and stands were already jammed. It was a Saturday morning in late June, the kind of day folks in this southeastern corner of New Hampshire might be putting in their last tomato plants or heading down to Boston to take in a Red Sox game. The parking lot had started filling up before the early morning fog had lifted. People had come from Londonderry and Hollis and Boston. There were young families pushing strollers, packs of college kids, and scores of seniors.

Kevin and Catherine Bauer had driven the twenty miles from Westford, Massachusetts, to hear the senator who wanted to be president. Both are software engineers. They liked that Sanders stands up for working people, that he's genuine and sticks to his beliefs, and that he doesn't take money from Wall Street. Asked whether they were concerned that Sanders might win the Democratic nomination but lose the general election, Kevin responded, "Nope—not really."

The Bauers, like many in the audience, were drawn to Sanders's core message: The billionaire class is controlling American politics; the middle class is getting screwed; and it will take a political revolution led by millions of ordinary

Americans to change the nation's course. As he warmed up in the Nashua Community College gym, he didn't disappoint.

"In Vermont and New Hampshire," Sanders said, his voice rising to a harangue, "families are working not one, not two, but three jobs to cobble together enough money for food, rent, and health care.

"That's immoral!

"That's unconscionable!

"That's un-American!"

The crowd jumped to its feet. Cries of "Bernie! Bernie! Bernie!" rose to the rafters.

Barely two months into his campaign Sanders had command of his basic stump speech, and it was more than enough to inspire crowds nationwide. His audience members were "bruthuhs and sistuhs," and the "rigged economy" was robbing them of wages and opportunity. The Keystone pipeline was a "yooooge mistake," and "the top one-tenth of one percent owns as much wealth as the bottom ninety percent." Republican family values meant women shouldn't have the right to control their own lives when it comes to contraception, and "most of us think that's insane." Sanders's family values meant guaranteed family medical leave, especially for new mothers. "If bonding with a newborn is not family values, I don't know what is!"

Sanders never saw a trade pact that didn't drain American jobs into other countries. He would pay for a free college education for all by taxing hedge-fund transactions and windfalls. He would come up with $1 trillion to rebuild bridges, roads, and rail lines and put a million people to work.

"This is not a democracy, it's an oligarchy," he repeated to every crowd's delight. "And it has to stop!"

★ ★ ★

Sanders's speech in Nashua was the first of six stops over two days in New Hampshire. He hit a fundraiser in a tent set up in the backyard of a wealthy immigration lawyer in Bow, a horsey enclave between Manchester and Concord; he stopped by New England College in the lovely village of Henniker. On Sunday he regaled smaller, more intimate, but equally enthusiastic gatherings at an inn in Rochester, at Oyster River High School in Durham, and at a lodge in Laconia.

The message remained constant, as did Sanders's uniform, a blue button-down cotton shirt, no tie, dark slacks, and dark brown shoes, and as did his demeanor: dark, determined, didactic. The package was working well. While he was ranging through southern New Hampshire, his poll numbers showed him gaining on Clinton, the clear frontrunner thus far. CNN released a poll showing 35 percent of respondents favoring Sanders and 43 percent Clinton. Sanders's popularity was inching up in Iowa as well.

Voters seemed to be attracted to Sanders because of his message and his inability to be anything but who he is: a Brooklyn guy on a crusade. When they got close enough, they were corralled by two skilled, experienced political teams from Vermont and Washington. The Vermonters had been with Sanders for decades and knew his quirks; the DC staffers were political professionals thrilled to be working for a true believer whose views they shared. "We see a path forward," Tad Devine said a few weeks after Sanders launched in Vermont. "We've been surprised by the depth of enthusiasm."

More than a few Washington political insiders were

surprised that Devine had signed on with Sanders. Devine is about as deep into the Democratic political consulting community as one can get. He's helped Democrats in almost every presidential campaign since Jimmy Carter's run in 1980. He handled delegates for Walter Mondale's primary and general election campaigns in 1984. He then worked for Mike Dukakis's presidential race and managed Senator Bob Kerrey's presidential campaign. For Al Gore and Joe Lieberman he served as senior strategist, and he did the same for John Kerry in 2004. "Devine is considered one of the leading experts on the Democratic Party's presidential nominating process and general-elections strategy," according to Harvard's Institute of Politics.

"See how Walter Mondale beat Gary Hart in the primaries," Devine says. "It's an inside game of politics and maneuvering. It takes money. It takes work."

Winning a national campaign in 2016 takes a strong presence in social media. Barack Obama's 2008 victory over Hillary Clinton was powered in great part by the groundbreaking social media operation crafted by Revolution Messaging. Revolution remains perhaps the best firm for social media, online advertising, online fundraising, web design, and digital advertising. Revolution went with Sanders.

"Like a lot of Obama supporters," Revolution's founder Scott Goodstein said in a statement, "we were looking for a candidate with a track record of doing the right thing—even if it meant taking on Wall Street billionaires and other powerful interests. A candidate who could inspire a movement."

Goodstein's canned comment is more revealing for what it doesn't say. He was one of many Obama supporters of the progressive ilk who were disappointed by President Obama's unprogressive record in his first term. Like many others, Goodstein sat out Obama's 2012 campaign. Now they were dedicating their considerable expertise to the much more progressive Sanders. When Sanders touts the hundreds of thousands of people who have contributed small sums to his campaign online, look to Revolution. Likewise the Sanders brand has a deep presence on Twitter, Reddit, Facebook, and Pinterest—thanks to Revolution. The last time Revolution went head-to-head with Hillary Clinton, its candidate won.

Sanders's Vermont staff is led by Jeff Weaver, a Vermonter with a generous girth and a very close relationship with the candidate. Weaver first met Sanders in 1986, when the Burlington mayor was running for governor. He later joined Sanders's congressional staff, rose to the top job, managed his successful 2006 Senate campaign, and ran the Senate office until 2009. Weaver left his business, Victory Comics in Falls Church, Virginia, to manage his friend's presidential campaign. The campaign's field director, Phil Fiermonte, is another Vermont native and has known Sanders for more than three decades; he has managed several of his campaigns and has directed his state operations for years. Then there's Jane O'Meara Sanders, the candidate's wife, who weighs in on most important matters.

The staff's small size, devotion to their candidate, and unparalleled expertise make for an agile operation. It can react to political events, pivot quickly, capitalize on opportunities, and avoid pitfalls.

"Bernie's message is really selling," Devine says in June 2014. "There is no polling at this point. Bernie strenuously resisted it. I find it very frustrating. If you want to run a modern campaign, you have to use modern tools."

Instead of polling, Sanders spent a year touring the country and personally testing his message in town hall settings. "It was unscientific," says Devine, "but he knew that when he talked with people all over the country and heard their reaction, his message was for real. There seems to be an extraordinary appetite for this kind of campaign driven by issues and substance rather than garbage." Devine was surprised by the strength of Sanders's early fundraising success. He started hauling in tens of millions of dollars in small doses from many people, thanks in part to Revolution's social media campaign.

This highlights another factor that gives weight to Sanders's ability to stay in the presidential race for the duration: he's incredibly frugal. He hates to spend cash. He hoards contributions. He keeps his staff small, advertises only when necessary, and travels light. He flies economy class. He shows up in a Ford Fiesta. With a yellow legal pad.

★ ★ ★

Sanders arrived at the Phoenix Convention Center on the evening of July 18, 2015, to deliver his first speech in Arizona. Nearly 11,000 people had crowded into the hall.

"Whoa," he said as he surveyed the smiling faces and "Bernie!" signs. "There are a lotta people here. A lotta. I cannot believe this crowd."

Neither could the political media believe the crowds coming to see Sanders and hear his diatribes against the billionaire class. They could not fathom why the "socialist senator from

Vermont" was attracting numbers ten times greater than Clinton's. The massive turnouts simply did not fit into their expectations of how the presidential campaign was supposed to play out. Journalists dutifully reported the mounting numbers: 11,000 in Phoenix, 8,000 in Dallas, 28,000 in Portland, Oregon. In Los Angeles on August 11, 27,000 people jammed the Memorial Sports Arena, and thousands more watched Sanders on Jumbotron screens outside the venue.

It was Sanders's first foray into friendly and unfriendly territory west of the Mississippi. "When we said we were coming to Arizona, someone said Arizona is a conservative state," he told the crowd. "What were they talking about?"

Texas is one of the most conservative states in the union on matters of gun rights, immigration, workers' rights, and gay rights. Yet when Sanders scheduled a July 20 appearance in Houston, organizers had to find a larger hall to accommodate the hordes. In 100-degree heat, an overflow line of 500 waited to get into the 8,000-capacity basketball arena at the University of Houston. By contrast, Clinton had drawn around 1,000 the month before a mile away at Texas Southern University.

Kenny Rogers, a fifty-eight-year-old schoolteacher with Houstonians for Sanders 2016 was handing out "Join the Revolution" flyers. He tried to explain to a reporter from the London *Guardian* the Vermonter's draw: "Something is happening out here. This is blowing me away, quite frankly. Houston is such a conservative town." In previous Democratic campaigns he had found organizing in Houston difficult. "This is not difficult."

At each venue Sanders delivered the same basic message

about the greed of bankers and the struggles of the middle class. But in Phoenix he began to change it up. He broadened his reach to throw his progressive beam on LGBT issues, reached out to his "gay bruthuhs and sistuhs," spoke out for women's reproductive rights and the environment. Egged on by activists with Black Lives Matter who interrupted his address at a Netroots conference in Phoenix, he added the need for criminal justice reform. But always returning to the heart of his campaign, he hammered away at the economic issues of workers' rights, income inequality, and the outsized power of the superwealthy.

As Sanders built to the crescendo of his Dallas speech and whipped the crowd of mostly students into a fine froth, he hit on one of his trademark proposals: "to make every public college and university tuition-free." Rick Perlstein wrote in the *Washington Spectator*, an independent, progressive publication:

> The crowd's response is so ecstatic it overdrives my tape recorder. It continues into a chant: BERNIE! BERNIE! BERNIE!
>
> And when the show ends, a crowd in a nearly post-coital mood of sated exhilaration doesn't want to leave, doesn't leave, until Bernie returns to the podium for something I've never witnessed at a political event, an encore, and announces that the crowd numbered 6,000.

★ ★ ★

What drives "Berniemania" in the run-up to the primary season? Bernard Sanders is a seventy-four-year-old old Jewish guy from Brooklyn with the unmistakable accent to prove it. He has the sartorial style of an economics professor, the political rhetoric of Eugene Debs, and the visage of your angriest uncle. How has he gotten this much traction, ascending to adoration, from coast to coast?

For one thing, Sanders comes as he is: unvarnished, un-handled, and genuine. He doesn't try to hide his Brooklynness, so perfectly lampooned by comedian Larry David on *Saturday Night Live*. He is an avowed Democratic Socialist and does not shy away from the deeply held, left-wing beliefs he's been harping on for the past fifty years. Contrast that with the fact that most Democrats fled from being branded liberal—the "L-word"—a decade ago.

"He's never changed his tune," says Andy Snyder, a Vermont activist, former legislator, and state education official who's worked with Sanders for years. "No one can accuse Bernie of saying what others want to hear. Nobody can accuse him of being disingenuous."

At a time when many political leaders are shifty, hedge their bets, dodge questions, and change their rhetoric based on the latest polls, Sanders is the antidote: authentic, unapologetic, and consistent. That in itself appeals to many voters, whether or not they agree with him.

Take Paul Wuerker. He and his wife, Judy, drove from Massachusetts to hear Sanders speak at Oyster River High School in Durham, New Hampshire. The Wuerkers, both in their sixties, beamed after hearing Sanders plead for "millions of Americans to stand up" against the billionaires. "I'm in," Judy Wuerker says. "A political revolution is only common sense."

The Wuerkers both work—she at the local high school, he at the electrical contracting company he owns. Thanks in part to high health care costs and their children's heavy college debt, they feel they can't retire.

Paul, a big, quiet fellow with a gap in his smile, didn't have much to say but offered this impression of Sanders: "I like what he has to say and how he says it. Even if I don't agree, he's straightforward and believes what he says."

But being a small-businessman, he must not buy into Sanders's take on workers and wages?

"I believe that we can have a small government that works for everyone," he replies. "Call me a Republican Socialist."

Beneath Sanders's authentic demeanor and delivery, his core canon about workers getting stiffed in a system controlled by an "oligarchy" of wealthy families strikes a chord among many voters, like the Wuerkers. Members of the middle class are struggling. Families are saddled with debt. Republicans increasingly seem to unabashedly and aggressively favor the wealthy. Sanders fearlessly addresses these concerns. "The world has come around to see things like he does," Fiermonte tells me. "Through the same lens."

Sanders began to acquire that bedrock worldview in Brooklyn during the 1950s and 1960s, when life was precarious for the middle class, especially for the Sanders family.

TWO

RADICAL ROOTS

"Virtually every member was murdered by Nazis."
—BERNIE SANDERS on his father's family

Midway through Sanders's senior year at James Madison High School in Brooklyn he quit showing up for track practice.

"He was a tremendous runner," says his teammate Lou Howort, who ran a leg in the distance medley relay with Sanders and Dan Jelinsky. "We were great together. Bernie ran the longest leg. We won our race in the Penn Relays." Then "Bernie got distracted by something. He started missing practices and seemed to lose interest."

Sanders had grown up playing sports on the streets and playgrounds of Madison Park, a neighborhood close to Sheepshead Bay on Brooklyn's south side. Every day after school and on weekends he and his buddies would play handball against the brick buildings or stickball in the street or baseball in a vacant sandlot. Sanders was always fast on his feet, and at Madison High he excelled on the track team and became co-captain. He was among the premier long distance runners in New York City.

Martha "Marty" Alpert was a regular track fan, a year ahead of Sanders at Madison. "I remember this tall, skinny kid— gawky, not a good-looking boy—but oh, my God, so fast," says Alpert, now president of Madison's alumni association. "It was rare to have six-footers at fifteen. His legs were very long."

Sanders even got a mention in a 1957 *New York Times* article. "His specialty was long-distance," Howort says. "We had a great cross-country team." The races were held on a hilly, two-and-a-half mile course in Van Cortland Park, way up in the Bronx.

Through friends Howort finally found out why his teammate no longer came to the track. Sanders's mother, Dorothy, was very sick, and he was spending every day after school and Saturday race days at home with her. "It wasn't as if everyone knew about it," says Howort. "Bernie was a reserved person. He kept it to himself."

The rising track star, it turned out, was more devoted to his mother than to the competition and acclaim he had begun to enjoy. He learned at an early age about sacrifice, the pain of loss, and the rewards of caring for someone you love.

"Bernie was a serious, honest person," says Howort, who, after Madison and college, taught health and physical education in New York public schools for decades and still lives in Brooklyn. "That was never questioned."

★ ★ ★

Sanders has never been forthcoming about his roots. He prefers not to dwell on his early family life, what shaped him, his victories and defeats. How the lifelong politician developed his core beliefs about the way the world should work—socialism—remains a mystery.

"He hates talking about himself. He thinks it's a distraction from what journalism should be about: serious issues, not, as he puts it, gossip," writes journalist Rick Perlstein, who's interviewed Sanders a number of times.

His reluctance to share his life story sets him apart from most politicians. Leaders and would-be leaders are usually eager to pen memoirs and paint gauzy portraits of their early struggles so they can "connect" with voters. Obama wrote two books that described his upbringing and the development of his worldviews. When Clinton wants to soften her image as a hard-edged political operator, she harkens back to her mother's difficult childhood and the way that struggle affected her own life.

"The usual path is to begin with biography," Sanders's advisor Tad Devine told the New York *Observer*. "I don't see us going there."

In his 1997 book, *Outsider in the House*, Sanders devotes three pages to his early life in Brooklyn. The bare facts give tantalizing hints about the factors and forces that shaped him. Every time a journalist pressed him for details, he parried that his personal story was insignificant and irrelevant compared to the collective problems facing the country. Focusing on his own history might detract from the serious work that needed to be done to correct the myriad injustices afflicting the working class.

But as the writer and activist Greg Guma told Sanders when he first ran for office in 1972, "You're asking people to vote for you. They need to know who you are, where you came from, what you believe in."

Sanders scoffed at the advice.

★ ★ ★

Sanders's father, Eli, came from Słopnice, a small village in Poland southeast of Krakow, not far from the border with Slovakia. He left the village with his brother and arrived in the United States in 1921 at the age of seventeen. Eli spoke Polish and Yiddish but not a word of English. Most likely he adopted the name Sanders at his point of entry, perhaps Ellis Island.

Eli had plenty of reasons to leave his home in Eastern Europe. The years after World War I were tumultuous in many countries bordering Russia; they were especially dangerous for Jews. Marauding soldiers from the White Russian Army allied with the czar attacked and killed Jews in Ukraine and Poland. Many soldiers with the revolutionary Red Army carried out pogroms to harass and cleanse the towns of Jews. When the Poles went to war with Ukraine and Russia, the Jews came under attack from both sides.

The Jews of Słopnice and Limanowa, a larger town to the north, suffered horribly under the Nazi occupation of Poland during the Holocaust. The Nazis occupied Limanowa on September 10, 1939. Two days later they shot twelve Jewish leaders, according to multiple accounts. *The Encyclopedia of Jewish Life before and during the Holocaust* recounts the fate of Jews in the region in 1942: "In June of the same year 1,500 Jews (of whom 600 were refugees) were placed into a ghetto and on August 18, after the Nazis murdered 160 of the old and sick, the rest were marched to Nowy Soncz for subsequent deportation to the Belzec extermination camp."

Auschwitz, perhaps the most infamous extermination camp, lay less than one hundred miles to the west of Słopnice. Bernie Sanders has said only that most of his father's family perished in the Holocaust, so he had few, if any, relatives on that side.

Asked about his Jewish upbringing at a breakfast session hosted by the *Christian Science Monitor* in June 2015, Sanders said it taught him "in a very deep way" what politics is all about: "A guy named Adolf Hitler won an election in 1932. He won an election, and fifty million people died as a result of that election in World War II, including six million Jews. So what I learned as a little kid is that politics is, in fact, very important."

The Brooklyn that Eli Sanders arrived in was a hurly-burly mix of immigrants fresh off the boat. Italians, Irish, Greeks, and Jews were competing to scratch out a living and survive in the New World. They clustered into well-defined neighborhoods, stayed within their borders, and inched toward assimilation. Eli wound up selling paint, at first perhaps from a pushcart. His son remembers him peddling paint as a traveling salesman working out of Long Island.

A few years after he arrived, Eli married Dorothy Glassberg. She came from a large Russian Jewish family on New York's Lower East Side, according to Sanders's profile in *National Journal*. She graduated from high school in the Bronx. Given her age and origins, it's more than likely that Dorothy was born in the United States, which made her a first-generation

American, one step closer than Eli to grasping the American Dream. They had their first son, Larry, in 1933. Bernard was born on September 8, 1941.

Sanders lived with his parents and brother at 1525 East 26th Street in a plain, beige-brick apartment building. It was—and still is—on the corner of East 26th and King's Highway, the neighborhood's main thoroughfare. Like a Lower East Side tenement, the building has a black metal fire escape zigzagging down its six-story front, a small entry foyer with a fake fireplace, and air-conditioning units sticking out of many windows. In the 1950s the building was occupied almost entirely by Jewish families. The Sanders unit had three and a half rooms. The younger boy sometimes shared a very small bedroom with his brother, or they took turns sleeping on the living-room couch.

When Sanders recalls growing up in the Brooklyn apartment, he never mentions love or caring, happy times or shared family rituals. "I grew up in a lower-middle-class home," he wrote in *Outsider*, "and knew what it was like to be in a family where lack of money was a constant source of tension and unhappiness."

In the book *The Jews of Capitol Hill: A Compendium of Jewish Congressional Members*, Sanders is quoted as saying, "It's not that we were poor, but [there was always] the constant pressure of never having enough money. . . . The money question to me has always been very deep and emotional."

Eli was the enforcer; Dorothy yearned to move out of the cramped apartment building and raise her family in her own home.

"Almost every household purchase—a bed, a couch, drapes—would be accompanied by a fight between my parents over whether or not we could afford it," Sanders wrote. "On one occasion I made the mistake of buying the groceries that my mother wanted at a small, local store rather than at the supermarket where the prices were lower. I received, to say the least, a rather emotional lecture about wise shopping and not wasting money."

Beyond describing his father as a paint salesman working "day after day, year after year," Sanders doesn't talk or write much about him. Eli's view of the world was shaped by growing up a Jew in Słopnice and sharpened by his transatlantic voyage with his brother to a new land. He was an Old World Polish guy trying to keep himself and his family in food and clothes. If he was like many other immigrant fathers of the time and place, he was frugal with money and tough on his family. "He wasn't a friendly guy," Sanders's friend Steve Slavin says of Eli. "Bernie rarely talked about it, but he didn't get along with him. He was much closer with his mother." Slavin's own father was so difficult that Slavin left home right after high school.

Lou Howort's father was also an immigrant; Lou sensed that he was torn between his European past and his American present: "He treated his family with an iron fist, like he was still in the Old Country. It led to some emotional and physical brutality. They came as immigrants. They didn't know anything else."

★ ★ ★

To get to P.S. 197, which he attended from kindergarten through the eighth grade, every morning, Sanders would turn right outside his apartment house and walk three blocks up Kings Highway. The Madison Park Hospital was on the right and his elementary school to his left, three blocks away toward Ocean Avenue.

The majority of the students at P.S. 197 were Jewish; the schoolyard took more space than the building; and the basketball courts were Sanders's home away from home. He grew taller and grew to love the game. Basketball was so popular, Steve Slavin recalls, that one of the teachers organized an afterschool league. In the eighth grade Sanders played on the Brooklyn Borough championship team.

After World War II the "Red Scare" spread fear that Soviet Russia would drop an atomic bomb on the country, and Sanders and his classmates practiced ducking under their desks during nuclear attack drills. But Brooklyn in the 1950s was homey and hopeful. The Allies had won the war. Former general Ike Eisenhower was in the White House; Richard Nixon was vice president. There was peace in the streets—if you didn't venture too far from your neighborhood.

"Brooklyn was like a collection of villages," says Larry Hite, a classmate of Sanders's. "Five streets over you would find different people, different culture, different food. . . . Where we lived was essentially a shtetl. We lived in a Jewish box, with a Jewish sense of humor, Jewish food, Jewish holidays. This is what Bernie took in. All that cultural stuff shaped him."

Up Kings Highway there were Jewish bakeries and candy stores, Dubrow's 24-hour cafeteria, and the Nostrand Movie Theater, the largest of four local film venues. When Sanders could scratch up a few cents, he would sneak over to the Nostrand with his brother or friends. At an early age he already had a love of film.

Whether he developed a love of Judaism is an open question. Brooklyn's central neighborhoods—from Brownsville and East New York to East Flatbush, Midwood and Sheepshead Bay—were predominantly Jewish, with a few Irish and Italian precincts scattered among them. When Sanders was coming up in the 1950s, there were ninety-one synagogues spread through the borough, according to *The Lost Synagogues of Brooklyn*.

"Being Jewish has greatly influenced my intellectual and emotional development," Sanders acknowledged to political scientist Steven Soifer in a 1985 interview.

Like most of his buddies, Sanders attended Hebrew school twice a week in the afternoon and again on Sunday. He studied the Torah, learned the stories of Abraham and Moses, Jonah and Jacob. He read about Israelites being enslaved in Egypt. In 1954 he became Bar Mitzvah, at the Jewish Center of Kings Highway, according to *The Jews of Capitol Hill*, most likely at a Reform temple, since his parents were not devout. In an interview with *Tablet*, a daily online publication of Jewish news, culture, and ideas, Larry Sanders said he and his brother didn't necessarily ascribe religious significance to Bible tales and parables, but they definitely derived a sense of right and wrong from the stories, as well as notions of justice, leadership, and revenge. The older brother explained that scripture "was encountered on an unintellectual level, but nonetheless it went very deep. We did not distinguish Jewishness from being American."

Cultural Jewishness came with a certain set of stories, standards, and expectations set by the immigrant Jews. They told tales about life in the Old Country, but they wanted their children and their children's children to achieve and prosper in the new land. They wanted their children to follow the faith, marry a Jew, and teach their children to be Jews. Valuing education as much as religion, they drove their children to excel in school, in hopes that each would become a professional: a teacher, doctor, lawyer, perhaps a dentist. "Our parents were interested in their kids getting a good education and going forth," says Marty Alpert, Sanders's Madison High schoolmate. "There was no question that we were expected to go on to higher education."

But being Jewish in Brooklyn in the 1950s had its limitations. Within their neighborhoods all their friends, the small businesses, the teachers and doctors were Jewish. When Jews ventured beyond the borders of Brooklyn, even past the lines that separated one neighborhood from the next, they often found themselves being harassed.

"We felt the hostility in different ways," Howort explains. "My father told us one day he had a job in Prospect Park and parked his car on the street nearby. Someone came out of the house and said, 'Get out of here, you Jew bastard.'"

Myron Kalin, another of Sanders's high school classmates, lived just beyond the Jewish neighborhood in a block that was mostly Italian. "I would get beat up on the way to school," he says. "They told me if I was very good, I would go to purgatory."

Says Larry Hite, who went on to great success managing hedge funds, "It was hard for a Jew to break into business. My father heard the phone company was hiring, so he applied for a job. They chose him out of the applicants and told him he was going to 'love it there.' When he was filling out his papers, they asked him which church he attended. He said he went to temple. They said, 'Oh, the job has been filled.'"

Sanders never mentions anti-Semitism. It was out there, beyond Madison Park and the "shtetl," but he rarely ventured forth. But he did take away a memory from his family and being Jewish that marked him for life.

"I very vividly remember my father . . . going through an album of family photos," he told an interviewer in the mid-1980s. "Virtually every member was murdered by the Nazis. Rather than religious training, the fact that my parents' families had been destroyed by a government had an enormous impact on me."

★ ★ ★

From all accounts Sanders adored his mother and didn't get along very well with his father. But the person who had the most influence in shaping him was his brother. "It was my brother, Larry, who introduced me to political ideas," Sanders wrote in *Outsider in the House*.

In an interview with the journalist Louis Berney for the *Vermont Vanguard* newspaper in 1981, Sanders said Larry had a "great influence" on his childhood. "Books and intellectual ideas were not topics of discussion with my parents. My brother brought books into the house. He introduced me to poetry and brought Sigmund Freud and political ideas home with him. He was the gateway for many intellectual ideas."

Larry Sanders made his kid brother tag along to meetings of the Young Democrats at Brooklyn College. He was the group's president, according to *Tablet*. Early on, members of the group joined a drive to stop an urban-renewal project on New York's Lower East Side that would force out lower-income residents. With his kid brother in tow, Larry went door-to-door in their neighborhood to collect signatures on a petition opposing the project. Despite their best efforts and a successful campaign, they failed to block the project. But Bernie got his first taste of activism.

Leftist politics were ingrained in Jewish culture, according to many of Sanders's contemporaries. "There were a lot of left-leaning Jews," says Hite. "Jews were on the outs. They knew what it was like to be downtrodden, what it was like to be rejected. They had suffered in the ghettoes of Europe. It gave them a leftist tilt. And Jews have a lot of empathy."

Says Walter Block, who ran on the track team with Sanders, "Most of our parents had escaped either from Hitler or the Soviet Union. Everyone just took that view." Block's own views gradually shifted. He's now a libertarian economist and professor at Loyola University in New Orleans, but in 1999 he told the *Austrian Economics Newsletter*, "In the fifties and sixties, I was just another commie living in Brooklyn."

Sanders's running buddy Howort recalls that there were many socialist organizations and unions in Brooklyn and New York at the time: "A lot of those groups came out of their experience in Europe. They got their members involved in public housing and protested evictions of low-income residents." Howort says politics, socialism, and activism were regular topics of conversation at the dinner table. "It was built-in in my case. For Bernie too."

Sanders says his family didn't discuss politics much, but he developed a sensibility that would fuel his own politics. "From earliest memories, I was a rebel and a non-conformist," he told political scientist Steve Soifer in a series of 1985 interviews. "Something that was with me ever since I was little was an instinct to not do what other people did because they did it."

★ ★ ★

Sanders's world expanded when he went to James Madison High, just down the street from his apartment building. Walking out the front door, he could see the track behind the school. His brother had graduated from Brooklyn College and left for Boston and Harvard Law School. That left Sanders alone in the small apartment with his father and mother, who was falling ill.

Madison High became his refuge.

"It was its own world," says Marty Alpert. "We had five thousand kids. It was bursting at the seams."

The student body was about 80 percent Jewish, the rest predominantly Italian and Irish. Sanders's classmates recall a few African American students, perhaps a dozen in the entire school. De facto segregation kept blacks on the other side of Eastern Parkway, three miles to the north.

Madison High School is renowned for the roster of famous alumni on the "Wall of Distinction" in the lobby just outside the auditorium. Among its graduates are Supreme

Court Justice Ruth Bader Ginsburg; New York senator Charles Schumer; singer Carole King; Stanley Kaplan, founder of the eponymous student testing empire; actor Martin Landau; comedian Andrew Dice Clay (born Andrew Clay Silverstein); and baseball great Frank Torre. Roy DeMeo, a member of the Gambino crime family, graduated with Sanders in the class of 1959. (Chris Rock attended Madison a few decades later but did not graduate.) Sanders's name would eventually be added to the Wall, but he was not a standout when he attended. "Each class had its geniuses, its brainy kids," says Myron Kalin. "I don't remember him being in that particular group."

Sanders wrote for the school newspaper, *The Highway*. He badly wanted to play basketball, and his failure to make the varsity team ranks "as one of the major disappointments of my life," he told an interviewer in Vermont. He switched to track and became a star right away. "He was one of the fastest freshmen in New York City," Howort says.

Kalin remembers Sanders "as a nice enough person. He was more on his own." The school had a number of social fraternities. "He didn't join any."

Howort remembers his classmate as a reserved, thoughtful person, not a guy who put himself out there. "He and I were never interested in the latest style, the latest fads. He didn't know [what the latest style was]. Neither did I."

Sanders did have political ambitions. He might not have been the most popular kid in his class of 1,200 seniors, but he campaigned to be their president. He lost to Kalin—but he paid Kalin a high compliment.

The Korean War had just ended, and Kalin had read that

children in Korea were "in terrible shape." In response he started a Madison High chapter of the Save the Children Federation. Every year the school collected funds and sent them to Korea, and Save the Children sent back photos and stories about the Korean recipients. Sanders worked with Kalin on the project. "It became my campaign platform," Kalin says.

It became very important to Sanders too. Under his school picture in Kalin's Madison High yearbook, Sanders wrote, "Of all the things that I've ever done at Madison, working with you on the Korean orphans program has been the most gratifying."

There was no guarantee that Sanders would go to college. His father had left school at a young age. His mother graduated from high school but never made it to college. When his brother, Larry, went to Brooklyn College, it was a family milestone. Following Larry, Sanders was determined to go beyond high school.

Harvard rejected him. That could have been the result of *numerus clausus*, or "closed number," Harvard's policy of limiting Jewish students to no more than 10 percent of the freshman class. The University of Chicago accepted him and offered a scholarship, but his mother's condition was worsening, so he decided to stay close to home. He matriculated at Brooklyn College, a well-regarded school a mile and a half north of Madison High, in Flatbush. Sanders considered the classes and professors subpar. "His heart was broken when Harvard turned him down," a classmate says.

When Larry moved back home briefly after graduating from Harvard Law, his younger brother felt cramped and looked for a place of his own.

The college freshman was also trying to figure out how to navigate the world beyond Madison High. In a revealing 1985 interview with writer Russell Banks for an *Atlantic* profile that never ran, Sanders gives a glimpse of his political awakening.

"Being a non-conformist, that was in me before I had politics," he told Banks. "But to give you an idea of just how politically naive I was, I remember like it was yesterday my first day at Brooklyn College, during orientation, right? There's this fair in the gymnasium where all the sororities and fraternities and student organizations have their literature and their people out. There was this table and this group called the Eugene V. Debs Club, and I said, 'What's that? I never heard of Eugene V. Debs.' and they said, 'Oh, we're the local socialists,' and I said, '*Socialists!*' I was shocked. Not that I was against it, you understand, but I was amazed. Here were real live socialists sitting right in front of me!"

Sanders didn't join the Debs club, nor was he enamored of Brooklyn College, but his year there was a crucial, transitional period into radical political thought.

Steve Slavin was not tight with Sanders in high school, but they both had run track and both had less than stellar relationships with their fathers. Slavin had left home and found a room for $40 a month in the home of a Madison High Latin teacher. When the larger attic room in the house became available for $80 a month, Slavin wanted to move in but needed a roommate. He heard Sanders was looking for a place, and they agreed to share the long room, which had a desk by the door and a couch along one wall. Sanders's bed was along the other wall; Slavin slept in the alcove. Sanders took a temporary job delivering mail before Christmas to help pay the rent.

"He was at the hospital with his mom a lot," Slavin says, "but I remember him going to the library virtually every night. He would take books out that had nothing to do with his courses." At the end of one semester Slavin asked him, "Why are you reading these books? We have final exams."

Sanders replied, "These books are much more interesting."

Slavin wound up reading a few. He remembers learning about the 1848 revolutions that toppled European monarchies and fostered an era of liberal rule and about the 1886 Haymarket bombing in Chicago that resulted in the jailing of union leaders accused of fomenting violence against police. Sanders turned Slavin on to the poet Vachel Lindsay, a traveling bard whose stanzas stood up for African Americans and lauded labor activists.

Sanders's favorite book was the biography of John Peter Altgeld, the progressive governor of Illinois from 1893 to 1897. Altgeld broke the Republican hold on the state house that had lasted since the 1850s. He signed workplace safety and child labor laws. He also pardoned the three surviving anarchists convicted in the Haymarket bombings. But he might be best remembered for refusing to allow federal troops to put down the Pullman Strike led by the socialist icon Eugene Debs. When the strikers disrupted delivery of the US mail, President Grover Cleveland offered to send troops to quell the strike. Altgeld argued against doing so, but Cleveland wound up sending the soldiers over the governor's opposition.

"Altgeld was one of his heroes," Slavin says.

Slavin remembers coming back to the room in a melancholy mood one night and picking up a book of short stories Sanders had taken out of the library. They were tales set during the Russian Revolution. One was a love story about two revolutionaries caught plotting to overthrow the government. The tale ends with their losing sight of one another as trains take them to separate Siberian prison camps. Another describes the three revolutionaries taken to the scaffold for trying to overthrow the czar. The one woman of the trio cries not because she's about to be hanged but because the two men were hanged first and she has to die alone. Slavin recalls, "They got me out of my depression."

Both young men shared leftist views and talked into the night about Supreme Court cases like *Marbury v. Madison*, which established the power of the courts to review and nullify acts of Congress. "We talked for hours about the intricacies of the case," Slavin says. "We were both real bullshit artists."

In June 1959 Dorothy Sanders passed away. With no reason to stay in Brooklyn any longer, Sanders made plans to move to Chicago and continue his education at the university in Hyde Park. His father died four years later, leaving Sanders an orphan in his early twenties.

★ THREE ★

THE ACTIVIST

"Make Love Not War."

Chicago mayor Richard J. Daley might have been the Boss, as columnist Mike Royko wrote, but at the start of the 1960s he was losing his grip.

Daley had delivered Chicago and the surrounding Cook County for the Democratic ticket and helped elect John F. Kennedy president. As the "kingmaker," he got a prime spot at Kennedy's inauguration and an invitation to 1600 Pennsylvania Avenue that evening. "We were the first family invited to the White House," he boasted on the way out.

But back in the Windy City unpredictable gusts awaited the mayor. While he was trying to avoid damage from massive police and public works corruption, the "Negroes," as they were called in those days, were getting restive. Thirty percent of black families in Chicago were squeezed into ghettoes and living in poverty, with a median annual income of $4,800. Years before the civil rights movement gained traction in the South and urban areas of the North, African Americans in Chicago started protesting discrimination. They organized marches against restrictive housing policies and lousy public schools. Community groups founded by the legendary community activist Saul Alinsky staged protests at City Hall.

When Eleanor Roosevelt suggested that northern cities set an example by beginning to desegregate neighborhoods, Daley responded, "I don't believe Chicago is as bad as some people say it is. We are making progress in race relations."

Neither Daley nor Roosevelt nor anyone else could foresee the massive changes that were about to wrench Chicago and the rest of the nation out of the quiescent 1950s and into the turbulent 1960s. The country was headed into a decade of protest, civil rights battles, assassinations, and cultural shifts. The Vietnam War would unleash passions that unnerved adults and gave birth to a counterculture beyond their control. Bob Dylan captured the moment when he crooned: "For the times they are a changin'."

Still, in 1960 Chicago was relatively calm. Daley ruled by patronage and managed to keep a lid on racial tensions. But if he had held a magnifying glass over the campus of the University of Chicago in Hyde Park he would have seen the first ripples of student unrest.

★ ★ ★

Sanders arrived in Chicago in 1961, moved his meager possessions and books into a dorm room, and started taking classes.

He survived on student loans, grants, and part-time work. It's safe to say he didn't relish his coursework or his professors. "I will not go down in history as one of the great students of the University of Chicago," he told a political symposium at the campus in September 2015.

Sanders wandered through academic pursuits. He started out majoring in political science. Then he ditched poli-sci for English. When reading and writing about the classics failed to grab him, he searched for another major. Eventually he drifted back to political science.

In his Madison High senior yearbook photo, Sanders's hair is short and neatly combed over from a part on the side, his thick, curly locks tamed for the camera. He wears a tan sport coat and a tie, a sweet smile but no glasses. He looks as though he is headed off to an Ivy League school. By the time he showed up in Chicago, he was wearing glasses with thick black frames, and the smile was gone. Tall and lanky, sporting ratty sweaters, he exuded purpose—but for what?

Ideas and ideals he'd gleaned from books by Freud and other writers in his brother's bookcase filled his head. His study of the populist John Peter Altgeld was fresh in his mind. The socialist politics that surrounded him in Brooklyn prepared him for the university's radical milieu. In Hyde Park he found comrades. More than a few were Jewish, progressive New Yorkers. All were primed for protest.

"I received more of an education off campus than I did in the classroom," he told *Time* magazine during the presidential primary campaign.

★ ★ ★

In 1960 Jim Rader moved to Chicago from Indiana, where he had grown up on a small farm. The American Friends Service Committee had hired Rader and his wife, Diana Maher, to direct its Chicago project house, located in Garfield Park, then a rundown neighborhood on the city's west side. The Quaker center would serve as a gathering place for community activists, political organizers, and progressive leaders passing through town. Rader and Maher lived upstairs and served as hosts for the workshops and meetings held in the house. "There was real political ferment in Chicago and Hyde Park," he says. "It was exciting to be part of it."

Rader would become Sanders's lifelong friend and eventually his staffer, but his earliest recollection of the future progressive leader was memorable for reasons other than activism: "The first time we met he went right to my two-month-old baby, picked her up, and held her. He was fascinated with her. I'll never forget that."

Waves of immigrants had flowed through Hyde Park, a neighborhood on Chicago's south side, about six miles from the downtown Loop. Jews settled there in the early twentieth century, just as they had in Brooklyn. African Americans followed, heading north in the Great Migration from the Deep South. In 1890 John D. Rockefeller chose Hyde Park for the site of the University of Chicago, which he endowed generously. The university attracted an active cultural community that included the screenwriter Ben Hecht, poets Carl Sandburg and Vachel Lindsay, and muckraker Upton Sinclair, the socialist author who exposed the horrendous working conditions of Chicago's meatpacking industry. Progressives like Clarence Darrow also made their homes in Hyde Park.

In the early 1960s the university provided opportunities to meet left-leaning leaders and socialists. Norman Thomas, the leader of the Socialist Party of America who ran for president six times, came to speak at the university and gave informal talks at the project house. The pacifist A. J. Muste often dropped by, and the civil rights activist Bayard Rustin, who organized the 1963 March on Washington, introduced students and activists to the tenets of civil rights, socialism, and the labor movement. "You had the opportunity to meet left-wing leaders of the ferment," Rader says, "many of whom called themselves socialists."

Sanders became more and more attracted to the socialist movement. He joined the Young People's Socialist League and attended meetings of the South Side Socialist Party. At the student center and the Quaker project house he joined heated discussions on nuclear disarmament, the impact of the Russian Revolution, how to implement socialism.

As a freshman, Sanders lived in Chamberlain House, a ponderous stone dormitory on the main quad. He tried to convince his roommate, David Reiter, that capitalism was a failed system that oppressed the majority, but Reiter was a disciple of conservative economics professor Milton Friedman. Sanders hated to lose. "I went to bed, but I have a vivid memory of him just sitting there, shaking his head, sadly," Reiter told *Mother Jones*. "He was so sad that I just couldn't understand what was wrong with the free market. It was more in sorrow than in anger."

On many campuses around the country in the early 1960s, students were beginning to learn about and practice leftist activism. Americans began hearing the term "sit-in." In one of the first well-reported protests of the civil rights movement, African American students staged a sit-in at a whites-only lunch counter in Greensboro, North Carolina, and touched off protests across the South.

Scenes from a country in Southeast Asia called Vietnam started to appear on TV screens. The country had been divided, and the communist North was fighting to reunify the nation under its rule. US leaders feared that a communist takeover would spread, and the "domino effect" would lead to communist domination of many more nations. Gradually the United States devoted more and more money and manpower to Southeast Asia. In October 1961 General Maxwell Taylor called for the first deployment of combat troops to Vietnam. US Army helicopter units arrived in Saigon months later. More US troops were deployed to the jungle nation, and images of Americans killed in combat showed up on the nightly news for the first time. The army began drafting young men, like Bernard Sanders, to fight a far-away war that few understood.

Colleges began to roil. The University of California at Berkeley, the University of Wisconsin at Madison, and Columbia University in New York soon became centers of student protests. But the University of Chicago had been a hotbed of radicalism for a decade. "The U of C had a reputation for radicalism during the 1950s," university librarian Ray Gadke told the *Chicago Tribune*. "During the Red Scare, a number of U of C faculty members were accused of being communists. That was the generation before Bernie was here, but there was still that reputation of being a red school when he was here."

In the early 1960s activists at the Hyde Park campus were

in the vanguard of many causes. Bernie Sanders, the kid from Brooklyn, often took the lead.

★ ★ ★

After his false start in academics, Sanders took a semester off. A dean suggested that he "reevaluate" his commitment to higher education. Translation: the kid from Brooklyn came close to flunking out of college. Rather than trying to take classes, Sanders repaired to the basement of the University of Chicago library, wandered among the stacks, and pulled classic tomes from the shelves. "That was probably the major period of intellectual ferment in my life," he told the *Vermont Vanguard* in 1981.

Sanders immersed himself in American and European history, philosophy, socialism, and psychology. He read Jefferson and Lincoln, Dewey and Debs. He absorbed Erich Fromm's psychology. He pored over original texts on communism and socialism by Marx, Lenin, and Trotsky. He studied Wilhelm Reich, the sexual evangelist and philosopher of free love who believed powerful orgasms could cure society's ills.

"It was a time of real searching," Sanders has said. The searching didn't necessarily propel him to higher achievement in his coursework. He would manage to graduate, but it's clear that the benefits he reaped from his time in Chicago did not come from Politics 101 or seminars in psychology.

He told the *Vermont Vanguard* that he spent a summer in southern California working at the state mental hospital in Orange County. "I became very interested in psychiatry and the relationship between mental illness and society," he said in the revealing 1981 interview. He started researching the "psychiatric aspects of cancer" and developed a theory that "disease, to a large degree, is caused by the way we live in society."

But Sanders was not cut out for medicine and psychiatry. He was cut out for proselytizing about free love and the sexual revolution. Infuriated by the university's strict student housing rules, which set curfews, barred women from living off campus, and restricted visiting in dorms by students of the opposite sex, he cut loose in a 2,000-word manifesto against forced chastity in the university's student newspaper, *The Maroon*:

> In my opinion, the administrators of this university are as qualified to legislate on sex as they are to mend broken bones. One can best use an old saying to describe their actions: that their ignorance of the matter is only matched by their presumptuousness. If they dislike sex, or if they think that it is "dirty," or "evil," or "sinful" that is their misfortune. It is incredible, however, that they should be allowed to pass their attitudes, or neuroses, on to the student body. . . .
>
> Not only must the administrators not be allowed to forbid students who desire sexual intercourse from being able to have it, but they must also not be allowed to prevent a man and a woman from spending a night in conversation, or from simply studying together, alone.

His conclusion: The "beauty and joy which love and sex is composed of can not be totally eliminated," but if the university restricts students from spending time alone in their dorms, "they will do it in motels, in cars, on the Midway, or behind the Chancellor's house—but they will do it."

Sanders's take on free love made national news and sparked a spirited debate, but it failed to change the university's policies.

★ ★ ★

The University of Chicago began expanding in the 1950s. It had designs on more territory in Hyde Park and was intent on steering the community's growth. The crime rate was rising in the area. Many down-at-heels neighborhoods were showing "urban blight"—planners' shorthand for shabby, poor, and black. The federal government was doling out multimillion-dollar grants for urban renewal. The university applied for grants and created the South East Chicago Commission to manage the renewal projects.

The 1960 census found that Hyde Park was 60 percent white and 40 percent black. The university promised to maintain that balance even as it renovated some neighborhoods. It hired William Zeckendorf of New York as the main developer. I. M. Pei came on as architect. There would be no "urban removal," as some city renovations were called.

The first sign of dissent appeared in the September 1961 issue of *Harper's* magazine, which ran an excerpt of urban activist Jane Jacobs's book *The Death and Life of Great American Cities*. She singled out a University of Chicago rehabilitation plan to bulldoze a commercial corridor along 55th Street and replace the storefronts with brick buildings for university housing and classrooms. The effect was to kill off the community's street life and turn it inward, thus ridding it of "blight."

The university defended its project and went even further, implementing a plan to buy buildings that were becoming majority black, turn them into student housing, and prevent white flight. Students said it was, indeed, "Negro removal." Again university leaders defended the practice, but when black students were turned away from renting university housing available to white students, student activists had had enough. "UC Admits Housing Segregation" was the headline in *The Maroon*.

Sanders had joined a number of activist groups on campus, including the Young People's Socialist League, but he took a leadership role in the Congress of Racial Equality, a radical offshoot of the NAACP. He became chair of CORE's social action committee. Organized by CORE, a mass meeting of students discussed the university's flawed policies and voted to mount a protest. Sanders, his co-leader Bruce Rappaport, and CORE directed the demonstrations during a frigid week in January 1962.

At noon on the appointed day students rallied near the steps of the administration building. Sanders mounted the steps and began to speak: "We feel it is an intolerable situation when Negro and white students of the university cannot live together in university-owned apartments." He then led the students into the hallway outside the university president's office. They sat down along the walls, pulled out books, read, and talked. At around 3:00 President George W. Beadle took the elevator up to the fifth floor, stepped out, and surveyed the thirty-three students occupying the hallway outside of his office. "Hi," he said, then walked into his rooms. The students stayed the afternoon and night.

The first civil rights sit-in in Chicago made national news. It lasted thirteen days, ending only when the administration and students reached a compromise agreement to form a committee that would investigate the matter. That might have been Sanders's first bad taste of compromise. He continued to hammer at the university in language presaging his calls for reform for decades to come.

"To attempt to bring about 'a stable interracial community' in Hyde Park without hitting, and hitting hard, the segregation and segregation mentality that exists throughout this city, is meaningless," he wrote in a 1963 letter to the *The Maroon*. "Hyde Park will never solve its racial problems, until the problems are solved throughout the city. Segregation (in the form of 'benign quotas'), the promise to white people that Negroes will not be freely admitted into the neighborhood, cannot work on any long-term basis." Sanders urged protestors to keep putting pressure on the university and criticized it for refusing to "discuss the failings of an economic system which, despite the great wealth of the country, does not provide adequate housing for large numbers of people."

Sanders and about forty other CORE members picketed the landlords of a university-owned building that refused to rent to African Americans. "Go back to your jungles," some people shouted at the protesters, according to the *The Maroon*. CORE also picketed a Howard Johnson's restaurant in Hyde Park when restaurant executives declined to adopt nondiscriminatory policies. During the time Sanders was a leader with CORE, the group organized a visit to campus by Malcolm X to speak on "integration or segregation."

By the time he was twenty-three, Sanders told *Time*, he had been arrested and fined $25 for resisting arrest while demonstrating to desegregate public schools in Chicago, had marched in Washington to protest nuclear disarmament, and had had a run-in with Chicago police.

In an incident that would have provoked activists with Black Lives Matter, *The Chicago Defender*, a black newspaper, published a photo of a Chicago cop twisting the arm of a young black woman. Sanders told Russell Banks that he and others had made a poster with the photo to announce a demonstration against police brutality, which he was posting around campus one afternoon.

"Unbeknownst to me," he told Banks, "a cop car was following along behind me, and as fast as I put the posters up, the cops were pulling them down. Finally, the cop car pulls up to me, and they get out and accost me."

Sanders was terrified. One of the cops jabbed a finger in his face.

"It's outside agitators like you who're screwing this city up," the cop says, according to Sanders. "The races got along fine before you people came here!"

The incident made Sanders late for a political science lecture on local government. "I saw right then and there the difference between real life and the official version," he told Banks. "And I knew I believed in one and didn't believe any more in the other."

The efforts of Sanders and other activists bore fruit. "UC

Ends Housing Segregation" was the front-page headline of *The Maroon* on July 19, 1963.

★ ★ ★

Leon Despres first ran for alderman of Chicago's 5th Ward, which includes Hyde Park, in 1955. A Progressive in the Debs mold, he promised to fight the Daley machine and reform the city's government. To which Alderman Paddy Bauler responded, "Chicago ain't ready for reform."

Running year after year on his progressive record, Despres served on the Board of Aldermen for twenty years. He was one of the few Independents on the fifty-person legislature and often the most liberal. In that time he crusaded to ban discrimination, preserve Chicago's landmark buildings from the wrecking ball, and gain equality for African Americans. He was often the lone vote in 49–1 defeats, but he never veered from his progressive beliefs.

In 1963 Sanders put his class work at the University of Chicago on hold and volunteered in Despres's reelection campaign. Sanders has never spoken publicly about the details of his experience on the campaign, but it was his first time working in electoral politics. He could identify with Despres, who had traveled to Coyoacán, Mexico, in 1937 to visit Leon Trotsky in exile. Despres later said the visit "turned out to be one of the leading events of my life."

Despres stepped down from elective office in 1975, but he had a lasting impact on politics in Chicago and beyond. He led the independent political coalition that eventually helped elect Chicago's first black mayor, Harold Washington, in 1983. Marking his death in 2009, National Public Radio reported, "Some argue that he helped pave the way for the election of the country's first black president, Barack Obama, who cut his political teeth in the same Chicago neighborhood."

It's not a stretch to see Leon Despres as a model for Bernie Sanders, intellectually and politically. Despres adhered to his core beliefs in civil rights and fair housing despite his lone status in Chicago politics. He didn't mind losing 49–1 on votes that mattered to him. He refused to compromise. For Sanders, walking door-to-door in Hyde Park was a revelation, helping Despres win was his first political high, and watching him stand up for his progressive beliefs helped cement Sanders's own doggedness.

★ ★ ★

In June 1964 Sanders graduated—barely—from the University of Chicago with a degree in political science. After reading the works of Marx and other socialist thinkers, he came away with a firm intellectual undergirding of his core beliefs. He had tasted leadership, addressed crowds of eager followers, devoted himself to crusades that actually succeeded in effecting real change. He also worked briefly for the United Meatpackers Union.

Sanders and his girlfriend, Deborah Messing, decided to marry, and the two traveled back to New York.

One of Sanders's lasting impressions of Chicago might have come from campaigning for Despres, whom Mayor Daley had marked for political execution. "I was very impressed by

Richard J. Daley's Chicago machine," he told Rick Perlstein in a 2015 profile in the *University of Chicago Magazine*. He noted that Daley's patronage formula was "A city worker for every 200 voters." This was the political education that informed his approach as mayor of Burlington, Vermont.

★ FOUR ★

THE HIPPY

"Eat the rich."

In the spring of 1966 Steve Slavin joined a pickup basketball game on a playground in Greenwich Village. Who should show up but Bernie Sanders, his old friend and roommate from Brooklyn College. He was the same lanky kid with a decent jump shot and aggressive moves under the basket, but his hair had grown long. The curly pile of black ringlets stood out in what was called a "Jewfro"—the Jewish version of the Afro hairstyle popular among Black Power leaders like Angela Davis.

Slavin had been in the army and had lived in Atlanta for a short time; now he was back in New York. He asked Sanders what he was up to.

"I own some land in Vermont," Sanders replied.

"Does it have a house on it?"

"Nope," Sanders said. "Just a couple of shacks."

One summer after he graduated from the University of Chicago Sanders had paid $2,500 for eighty-five acres in Middlesex, a small town a few miles north of Montpelier, Vermont's capital. Slavin figured Sanders bought the property with his Bar Mitzvah money, along with some wedding cash. He also received a small inheritance from his father, who had died in 1963.

Sanders lived most of the year in New York, but he summered in Vermont. In the city Sanders bounced from job to job: he taught preschoolers for Head Start and worked as an aide at a psychiatric hospital. Around this time, early in the Vietnam War, Sanders applied for Conscientious Objector status, according to the Russell Banks profile. The only way to obtain CO status at that point was on religious grounds of opposition to all war. "There's nothing about being Jewish that says you can't shoot a gun," Sanders told Banks. His deferral was denied—after a series of hearings, an FBI investigation and numerous hearings, according to Banks—but by that time he was 26 and too old to be drafted.

The Vermont property was a hilltop meadow surrounded by woods with an old, run-down shack where farmers used to boil sap down to maple syrup. With no power and no running water, it was a step above camping out. "It was just fantastic," Sanders told Russell Banks in his *Atlantic* interview. "I mean, I grew up in a three-and-a-half-room apartment, never owned a damn thing, and owning a piece of land I could walk on was just incredible! This brook is *my* brook! This tree is *my* tree!" He found work researching property records for the Vermont Department of Taxes. For a time he registered people for food stamps at a nonprofit called the Bread and Law Task Force. A steady job was hard to find.

One summer Sanders brought three African American kids from New York to spend a couple of weeks in Vermont. It was his version of a Fresh Air Fund escape from the city. The problem was that there wasn't enough room in the sugar shack for Sanders, two boys, and a girl. He desperately needed to add space, or at least extend the roof so they had a simple shelter for a kitchen and dining room. Sanders wasn't much of a carpenter; fortunately he soon got help from an old friend who had grown up on a farm and knew his way around construction.

Jim Rader had left Chicago and moved to Plainfield, Vermont, where his wife could finish her degree at Goddard College. The alternative college was a free-for-all gathering place for hippies, searchers of truth, and anyone seeking a different approach to higher learning. One day Sanders ran into Rader's wife on campus. They reminisced about their activist days in Chicago.

"We renewed our friendship very easily," says Rader. When Sanders related his construction woes, Rader helped him buy the lumber and extend the roof into a decent overhang. "At least it was a place where they could cook and eat."

Meanwhile Sanders's marriage to Deborah had frayed. When Michael Kruse, working on a profile of Sanders for *Politico*, asked the senator's office staff about the first marriage, his press person said, "She got a Mexican divorce is what I was told."

Sanders started a relationship with Susan Campbell Mott, whom he had met in New York, according to Kruse. They lived together in New York and Vermont, but not on the Middlesex

land. In March 1969 Sanders bought another piece of property in the tiny town of Stannard, population 200, in a remote
corner of Vermont known as the Northeast Kingdom. Kruse
reported that a few days afterward Mott gave birth to Levi
Noah Sanders in St. Johnsbury, twenty miles down the road
and the nearest city with a hospital.

Mott and Sanders never married, but they lived together
for several years and cooperated in raising their son.

★ ★ ★

In Vermont during the hippy years of the 1960s and 1970s, relationships were perishable. For many of the young newcomers to the Green Mountain State, matching up, rematching,
and mating were not only accepted; they were approved. Stephen Stills released the hit song "Love the One You're With"
in 1970, but Vermont hippies were putting that into practice
a decade earlier. Having a child without hewing to society's
expectation that you get married first was not necessarily the
norm, but it was neither unusual nor disapproved of. Among
his fellow believers Sanders was merely practicing what he had
been preaching. After all, he had been advocating "free love"
since he read Wilhelm Reich at the University of Chicago,
when he had upbraided the administration in print for setting
curfews and restricting visitation in the dorms.

Hippies who wanted to go "back to the land" flocked to
three places at the height of the movement: Oregon, the Missouri Ozarks, and Vermont's Green Mountains. The 1960s
counterculture movement likewise coalesced loosely into three
separate tribes. The free-speech radicals were more purely

political; they were centered primarily in Berkeley and at New York's Columbia University. They demanded the freedom to protest on campus. In 1964 many joined dedicated civil rights activists on buses to Mississippi to register black voters during Freedom Summer.

The flower children made San Francisco's Haight-Ashbury famous as a place for hanging out and getting high. When Timothy Leary told crowds in Golden Gate Park in 1966 to "turn on, tune in, drop out," many hippies adopted his mantra. They were into taking drugs—pot, LSD, and hallucinogenic mushrooms—to expand their minds.

Vermont's "back to the land" hippies adhered to a slightly different ethos. They subscribed to *Mother Earth News* and *Organic Gardening*. The *Whole Earth Catalog* was their Bible for living, building, growing, preserving, fixing cars, and getting along with fellow hippies. Their ultimate goal was to become self-sufficient. Decades before doomsday "preppers" took to the far reaches of Idaho and prepared for Armageddon, Vermont hippies were going off the grid and creating what they considered to be a purer existence. There was a touch of the Utopian in the lifestyles they were creating.

Writing for *Playboy* in 1970, John Pollack estimated that there were 35,800 hippies in Vermont, and they accounted for nearly 33 percent of state residents between eighteen and thirty-four. He suggested they could soon take over the state. Governor Deane Davis hastily called a press conference to assure Vermonters that he hadn't invited all the hippies.

If you take away the Utopian conceit, the hippies were in concert with backcountry Vermont farmers, who were, of necessity, the epitome of self-sufficiency. When their tractors broke down, they had to become mechanics. When brutal Vermont winters blasted their homes, they warmed them with wood they had cut, split, and stacked. They ate from the gardens they tended and dined on the meat of deer they shot, butchered, and preserved. "Vermonters in the 1960s and '70s were mostly accepting of hippies because Vermonters are anti-authoritarian by nature," the Vermont Historical Society attributed to the *Rutland Herald* in 1983, "and traditionally accepting of radical groups and free thinkers."

Ultimately Vermont farmers just wanted to be left alone. As did the hippies. Once the farmers got accustomed to men with ponytails and women showing up braless in peasant dresses, they found common ground with the newcomers who wanted to go back to the land. They even hired the city kids, who could toss hay bales, feed cattle, and fell trees—for cheap.

Sanders had joined the migration of hippies, searchers, and dreamers to the Green Mountains and moved there permanently in 1968, then bought the land and settled in Stannard the following year. "My hair was long, but not long for the times," he told Mark Jacobson for a piece in *New York* magazine in 2014. "I smoked marijuana but was never part of the drug culture. That wasn't me."

★ ★ ★

Why Vermont? Why did Sanders decide to go back to the land in New England rather than join the free-speech radicals at Columbia? Schooled in the civil rights movement in Chicago, why go to a rural state where the sighting of an African American was a rare occurrence. The 1960 census reported that the number of nonwhites living in Vermont was 690 in a total population of 366,545. Why choose a state where there were so few socialists and leftists, let alone Jews?

Larry Sanders might have planted the Vermont seed when he took his little brother to see an exhibit in Manhattan about picturesque, cheap land in Vermont. It's certain that Sanders's desire for a rural, communal life was stimulated in part by his visit to an Israeli kibbutz in 1964.

In the summer of 1964 the Sanders brothers traveled abroad, separately. Larry was touring Europe; Bernie had wanderlust after graduating from the University of Chicago and wanted to rendezvous with his big brother. They decided to spend most of their time together in Israel. "It never occurred to us not to visit Israel," Larry told *Tablet* in 2014. "It was quite natural."

Sanders spent six months on a kibbutz. The word means "group" in Hebrew; the Kibbutz Program Center further defines it as "a voluntary democratic community where people live and work together on a non-competitive basis. Its aim is to generate an economically and socially independent society founded on principles of communal ownership of property, social justice, and equality." That could be a blueprint for the rural communities, or "communes," that hippies set up in Vermont, and the Center's description of kibbutzim could have described back-to-the-land hippies: "Their dream was not just to settle the land, but to build a whole new kind of society."

Sanders rarely mentions his time as a young man in Israel or the impact of living on the kibbutz. No one has been able to unearth the name of the kibbutz, though a close friend says it was one of the oldest. His brother says Sanders interrogated kibbutz leaders on their economic plans and was amazed that the men played a major role in family life and raising children—so different from his own upbringing. "The kibbutz was marvelous in that sense," Larry told *Tablet*. "People could do things in which they had no background whatsoever." Living on the kibbutz showed him and his brother that "you didn't need big bosses, you didn't need massive wealth" to live well, and socialism was something "that could work."

Sanders told friends that seeing Israelis grow vegetables that would sustain them made a huge impression on him, according to the *Tablet* article. He recognized the lifestyle as a "utopian form of existence," and he appreciated the agrarian, egalitarian nature of kibbutz life as a "less alienating form of labor" in the Marxist sense.

"What I learned, is that you could have a community in which the people themselves actually owned the community," he told the *Los Angeles Times* in 1991. "Seeing that type of relationship exist, and the fact that these units in the kibbutz were working well economically, made a strong impact on me."

No doubt when Sanders lived in Stannard he witnessed the kibbutz-like style of living in neighboring communes. Stannard was in Vermont's commune belt, close to Earth Peoples Park, a renowned commune near the Canadian border. He lived within range of other communal farms, such as New Hamburger Commune in Plainfield and Quarry Hill in Rochester. Sanders and his close friends say he himself never lived on a commune, but living in that place and time he surely experienced communal situations, even if simply sharing common living space. No one had the money or the desire to live alone; of necessity everyone shared.

★ ★ ★

While nearby hippies were hoeing vegetable beds, canning to-
matoes, and otherwise getting back to the land, Sanders went
back to the typewriter. In his ramshackle farmhouse on a dirt
road outside Stannard, he spent hours banging out rambling
essays on subjects ranging from cancer and public education to
the sexuality of children.

Drawing on the teachings of Wilhelm Reich that he had
embraced in college, he argued in an essay for the *Freeman*
that cancer may be caused by emotional distress. That was especially the case, he wrote, with breast cancer, which he attributed to sexual repression of young girls, referring often to
The Cancer Biopathy, Reich's 1948 book that proposed a direct link between emotional and sexual health, in particular
the dire consequences of suppressing "biosexual excitation."
Reich had patented the Orgone Box, with which users could
enhance their orgasms, the better to ward off cancer. The Food
and Drug Administration had banned the interstate shipment
of the boxes and jailed Reich when he violated the ban. He
died in jail in 1957.

At twenty-eight Sanders knit Reich's ideas into his fully
formed philosophy, conflating health and cancer with sex and
social mores. "How much guilt, nervousness have you imbued
in your daughter with regard to sex?" he asked in his essay.

If she is 16, 3 years beyond puberty and the time which
nature set forth for childbearing, and spent a night out
with her boyfriend, what is your reaction? Do you take
her to a psychiatrist because she is "maladjusted," or a

"prostitute," or are you happy that she has found someone with whom she can share love?

Are you concerned about HER happiness, or about your "reputation" in the community?

The provocative essayist also posed questions about public education:

With regard to the schools that you send your children to, are you concerned that many of these institutions serve no other function than to squash the life, joy, and curiosity out of kids? When a doctor writes that the cancer personality "represses hate, anger, dissatisfaction, and grudges, or on the other hand is a 'good' person, who is consumed with self-pity, suffers in stoic silence," do you know what he is talking about, and what this has to do with children, parents, and schools?

In a letter to the editor published by the *Freeman* in March 1969 that would please proponents of home schooling, Sanders ranted:

One of the most heartening signs in recent years is the growing belief among people that the formal education process (i.e., schools) are not only "not good" but that they are positively destructive and harmful. People are becoming aware that the function of schools is not to educate children but, in fact, to do the very opposite—to PREVENT education.

Later in the letter he wrote:

It is quite clear that the basic function of the schools is to set up in children patterns of docility and conformity— patterns designed not to create independent and free adults, but adults who will obey orders, be "faithful" un- complaining employees, and "good" citizens.

But Sanders was not a total downer. Yes, he was bummed out about the Vietnam War and many aspects of modern pol- itics. In the opinion pages of the *Freeman* he railed against "napalm, bombings, torture of whole villages," and "a United States congress composed of millionaires and state legislatures controlled by lobbyists." But he ended on an upbeat note:

The Revolution is coming, and it is a very beautiful rev- olution. It is beautiful because, in its deepest sense, it is quiet, gentle, and all pervasive. It KNOWS. What is most important in this revolution will require no guns, no commandants, no screaming "leaders," and no vicious publications accusing everyone else of being counter- revolutionary. The revolution comes when two strangers smile at each other, when a father refuses to send his child to school because schools destroy children, when a commune is started and people begin to trust each other, when a young man refuses to go to war, and when a girl pushes aside all that her mother has "taught" her and ac- cepts her boyfriend's love.

The revolution comes when young people throughout

the world take control of their own lives and when people everywhere begin to look each other in the eyes and
say hello, without fear. This is the revolution, this is the
strength, and with this behind us no politician or general
will ever stop us. We shall win!

Ultimately Sanders was unable to stay in Stannard. There
was no money in writing. The town may have been too remote for him and his infant son. He might have soured on
the communal lifestyle. Or his citified upbringing and college
life might have made him crave more human interaction. For
whatever reason, Sanders migrated to Burlington and had settled there by 1971. He and Levi moved into the back of a small
brick duplex at 295½ Maple Street, not far from the campus of
the University of Vermont.

According to friends at the time, Sanders struggled to
keep food in the refrigerator and lights on in the house. He
attempted to make money as a carpenter, with little success.
He sold a few freelance articles to low-budget publications.
"He was always poor," says Sandy Baird, who knew Sanders at
the time. He went on unemployment for a while in 1971. At
one particularly destitute moment, according to a friend who
lived around the corner, he couldn't pay his electric bill and
had to get his power by running an electric cord up from the
basement.

Levi's mother visited often to share in raising their son,
who called his father "Bernard."

★ ★ ★

When Sanders visited Burlington in early 1971, his friend Jim Rader let him stay in his apartment on North Winooski Avenue for a week or two. Then he rented an apartment on Front Street, not far from the rail yards along Lake Champlain and the police station. Rader was already plugged into the radical side of Vermont politics. He invited Sanders to a political fair at Middlebury College, where they attended a workshop led by two members of Liberty Union, a new political party that was in the formative stage. "Bernie joined a debate on whether it would be better for Progressives to work within the Democratic Party or build Liberty Union as a third party," Rader recalls. "Bernie defended Liberty Union as a separate, alternative party."

It was Sanders's first contact with Liberty Union. When Rader told him about a Liberty Union convention he planned to attend at Goddard College about a two hour drive east, near the town of Plainfield, Sanders said, "Let's go." He sat in the back of Rader's car with Levi on his lap, next to a girlfriend and her two little girls, and Rader at the wheel.

"Why did I go?" he asked in his political memoir, *Outsider in the House*. "I don't know."

A scrum was shaping up for Vermont's political officeholders. Senator Winston Prouty had just died, after being in office since 1959. Congressman Robert Stafford moved up temporarily to fill Prouty's place, which opened up Stafford's seat in the House. The race was on for the open House seat in a special election to be held in January. Stafford would have to run for the Senate seat. Vermont's population was so small it was allotted only one congressional seat along with its two Senate seats.

Rader, Sanders, and company made their way to a large room where a group of about 25–30 Liberty Union members was putting together the party's slate for the January special elections. Doris Lake, a newcomer to elective politics, volunteered to run for the House. But who would run for the Senate? The exchange went something like this:

"Is there anyone who can be lion bait for the Senate race?" asked John Bloch, one of the original organizers. "We need a body."

Silence. Party members swiveled their heads to see if anyone would volunteer.

"Sure," Sanders said, "I'll try it. What do I have to do?"

Rader looked wide-eyed at his friend. "It was a total surprise to me, but Bernie always had chutzpah."

Sanders stood up and spoke a bit about his views on education, the war in Vietnam, and the economy. He remained silent about his views on sexuality and health. As he says in his memoir, "I was chosen as the candidate unanimously because there was no competition."

So, on a lark, with no particular aim, Bernard Sanders became an official candidate for the US Senate. And because he was running in Vermont—a small, quirky state with a population of fewer than 400,000—it actually mattered. Had he been nominated or volunteered to run for the Senate in New York or Ohio or California, on the ticket of a party that was less than a year old, he might have been a footnote at best. Nowhere else could a relative newcomer with a baby on his lap, Orgone Boxes on his mind, and no prior political experience be taken seriously as a candidate for federal office.

Vermont was ripe for the Liberty Union Party and its

radical candidates. In the 1960s iconoclastic alternatives to the standard Democrats and Republicans, often called "people's parties," were making headway in California and other states. The Liberty Union Party had been founded in 1970 in a farmhouse in West Rupert. In the living room "young men and woman with long, tousled hair/anti-war activists from Marlboro College and old radicals, many of them urban dropouts," gathered to found a new political party, according to the official history. Former congressman William Meyer, the first Democrat ever elected to represent Vermont in Congress, hosted the meeting. The new party was founded to "boldly address their issues, the war in Vietnam, the militarization of society, the problems of the poor, and the destruction of the environment," the party's website proclaims.

By Vermont law a political party that gains more that 5 percent of the vote gains major-party status. Vermonters immediately took the new party seriously, invited its candidates to political forums, and allowed them to tour public facilities. All the media—TV, radio, and print—covered their speeches and events.

When a *Burlington Free Press* reporter asked Sanders why he was running, he responded, "The concentration of power makes the average man feel irrelevant. This results in apathy. As for my qualifications, I am not a politician."

That became abundantly clear when Sanders participated in his first call-in radio interview.

Rader recalls tuning into the program on his car radio. It sounded scratchy, but he was within range. "There was this rumble running through the whole interview," he says. In the Burlington radio studio Sanders was sweating and his legs were shaking. His knees kept hitting the legs of the table. The microphone was picking up the rapping sound, which went out on the airwaves as a constant thumping, like interference. Sanders couldn't figure out why the sound engineer kept frantically waving at him through the glass partition.

"Who is this guy?" one caller asked.

But Sanders soon got over his reticence to speak in public. He possessed a fundamental requirement for any prospective politician: he liked to hear himself talk. Reporters from Vermont's daily newspapers interviewed him when he showed up in Brattleboro or Rutland, Middlebury or St. Johnsbury. His take on the issues was reported on the front page. He called press conferences, and journalists actually showed up. Debate organizers invited him to join the panels to take on the Democrat and Republican candidates.

No one was as surprised by all this as Sanders. "Here I was," he told an interviewer in 2014, "running on this tiny party, with no money, but I was allowed to participate in the debates, I was on the radio, interviewed in the newspapers, actually taken seriously. Could you imagine that happening today?"

In the 1972 Senate race his first debate took place in the auditorium of Lyndon State College, in a small town not far from his former home in Stannard. Sanders faced off against Republican Robert Stafford and Democrat Randolph T. Major. Fewer than twenty people were in the audience. One was Rader. At one point the moderator asked the three candidates about the source of their campaign funds. When Sanders's turn came he pointed to Rader in the audience. "One of my major contributor is right there," he said. "He drove me here tonight." Sanders didn't have a car at the time.

Sylvia Manning met Sanders when he moved to Burlington and knew him as a single dad rather than a budding politician. "He wasn't freaky like the rest of us," she says. Manning was a Texan from the textile mill town of New Braunfels who had wandered to Vermont on a whim. "He was straight, even then. No pot. He wasn't a hippy. He was serious already." She had the sense that winning office wasn't her friend's ultimate goal: "He ran so he could get air time. Not to win but to educate people. He thought of himself as the educational candidate."

Sanders would often team up with Doris Lake, the other Liberty Union candidate, perhaps because she had wheels. They toured the state with their young kids. Sanders would walk into state prisons or high schools with Levi on his hip. Lake carried her daughter, Paula. Their tour of the control room of the Vermont Yankee nuclear reactor "spooked us both," Lake recalls. Their visits were more fact-finding missions than campaign stops to troll for votes. "If we went to a factory, we would interview the workers about their conditions and wages instead of asking for their votes." She adds, "People were very welcoming to having us speak. We were a legitimate party."

Sanders often lugged around a report written in 1970 by the staff of the House Banking Committee. It documented how some large American banks exerted inordinate control over many corporations. Quoting from the report in speeches and debates, Sanders would explain how "interlocking boards"

allowed a handful of powerful men to control entire industries and dominate the lives of millions of workers. "Time after
time," he writes in his memoir, "I pointed out that such disparity in the distribution of wealth and decision-making power
was not just unfair economically, but that without economic
democracy it was impossible to achieve genuine political democracy."

That was a short hop from the socialism Sanders adhered
to in his Chicago days, but he concluded that advocating economic and social justice was mainstream—then and now. He
also advocated legalizing drugs and widening entrance ramps
to highways to make it easier to pick up hitchhikers. These
ideas were not so mainstream.

In January 1972 Stafford won the race with 45,888 votes
to Major's 23,842. Sanders tallied 1,571 votes, 2.2 percent of
the total. But winning was far less important than imparting
his views, especially on economic justice.

No one who followed Vermont politics expected Sanders, or anyone running on the Liberty Union ticket, to win a
statewide election in the 1970s. The Green Mountain State
had been a reliable, rock-ribbed Republican fortress since the
Civil War. Before 1974 Vermonters had elected one Democrat
to statewide office. They overwhelmingly supported Ronald
Reagan in 1980 and 1984 and George H. W. Bush in 1988.
But underlying those Republican voting patterns, Vermonters
believed in a flinty kind of Libertarianism; they rejected hypo-
crites, respected authenticity, and honored self-reliance.

Sanders loved campaigning for senator. One could say
he had found his life's purpose: to campaign, to educate, to
preach. In the fall of 1972 he tossed his hat in the ring for

governor. He toured Vermont with Dr. Benjamin Spock, the famous pediatrician, who was running for president on the People's Party ticket. Democrat Tom Salmon became governor. Sanders barely broke 1 percent, polling 2,175 votes. He became chair of the Liberty Union Party.

In 1974 Sanders took a second whirl at the US Senate. He challenged Chittenden County prosecutor Patrick J. Leahy and Republican congressman Richard Mallary for the seat vacated when Senator George Aiken died. In his thirty-four years in the Senate, the salty Vermont farmer often broke ranks with the Republicans and favored liberal causes. At first he backed President Lyndon Johnson's war in Vietnam, but by 1966, as the news became grimmer and the cause less clear, Aiken suggested a way out for LBJ to "declare the United States the winner and begin de-escalation."

Sanders launched his campaign on a note that he sounded time and again—and yet again in 2015: rapacious capitalists and imperialists had pushed American society to the edge. "I have the very frightened feeling that if fundamental and radical change does not come about in the very near future that our nation, and, in fact, our entire civilization could soon be entering an economic dark age." In a letter to President Gerald Ford he warned that naming Nelson Rockefeller vice president would bring "a virtual Rockefeller family dictatorship over the nation."

Leahy won the Senate seat, but a record 5,901 voters punched Sanders's ticket, giving him more than 4 percent of the vote.

Sticking with his two-year cycle, Sanders ran for governor in 1976 against Republican Richard Snelling and Democrat

Stella Hackel. By then he had his debating points down pat, and he sharpened them for what would be his last run with the Liberty Union Party. During the televised debate he cut loose. Hunched over the dais, his dark curls falling over his forehead, he stared intently through his thick glasses and blasted his rivals for avoiding the issues that he said mattered most to Vermonters: better jobs, fair wages, and radical tax reform. He advocated doubling the corporate income tax and eliminating personal income tax for Vermonters making less than $10,000 a year. "The people of the state of Vermont have got to stand up to the two or three percent who control the money," he said.

Sanders lost, but he scored a personal best: 11,317 people cast their ballots for him, giving him 6.1 percent of the vote, and Liberty Union maintained its major-party standing. But Sanders was beginning to lose his zest for campaigning. He had run four times and lost four times. He wasn't earning any money. He was raising Levi and living hand-to-mouth. The Vietnam War was winding down, and Liberty Union was losing its purpose, at least in his view.

Almost a year after losing the governor's race, in October 1977 Sanders quit the Liberty Union Party, saying it had been "virtually dormant" since 1976 and calling it "a failure." He thought his political career was over. When reporters asked about his next move, he replied, "I don't know about my future."

★ ★ ★

Sanders might have been sick of campaigning and coming home to a bleak, ratty apartment, but he emerged from his

Liberty Union years with the essential ingredients for a successful career in elective office.

First, he had drummed the name "Bernie Sanders" into Vermont's political and media consciousness. He had started to build the Bernie brand, based on steadfast advocacy for workers against the interests of the wealthy few.

Second, he had found a core group of friends and advisors who would stay by his side in one form or another for forty or fifty years. Jim Rader was first among them. He had helped introduce Sanders to progressive ideas and leaders back in Chicago. In Vermont he drove Sanders to the Liberty Union session where he first volunteered to run for elective office. He drove him around the state for his first campaign. Over the next decade he continued to be a friend and political ally while he pursued his own career as a social services counselor.

John Franco was an impressionable student at the University of Vermont when he first saw Sanders in action in a church basement in 1974: "He was incredibly charismatic. He was speaking at the Liberty Union Convention. I didn't want him to stop." Since then Franco has never stopped helping Sanders, as an advisor, lawyer, and loyal staffer.

On the train from New York to Vermont on Labor Day 1976, Sanders sat next to a tall, big-boned fellow wearing a yarmulke who introduced himself as Richard Sugarman. He had just finished his doctorate in philosophy at Yale, where he had roomed with Joseph Lieberman, who would become a senator from Connecticut and a candidate for vice president. A devout Jew, Sugarman was on his way up to Burlington to start teaching religion classes at the University of Vermont.

He and Sanders talked. And talked. They were the same

age. Sanders had just come from a family reunion in Brooklyn. He told Sugarman it hadn't gone very well. "They don't get me," he said.

Sugarman got Sanders. Then he got Sanders and Levi: when Sanders couldn't pay his rent and the landlord evicted him from the house on Maple Street, he moved in with Sugarman.

For the next few years Sanders struggled to make a buck. He started an educational-film company with plenty of ideas but no cash. He couldn't separate himself from his socialist roots. He made his first and best video about his idol, Eugene Debs, the leader of the Socialist Party of America, who had run for president five times. The video was rough. Sanders and his partner couldn't afford to hire anyone to do the voice-over, so Sanders had to play Debs. In his Brooklynese, *workers* came out as "wuhkuhs" and *huge* as "yoooge." Debs was from Indiana.

Sanders drove from school to school trying to sell the Debs video and some educational slide shows. He was not finding success. He was nearing forty and had not had a regular paycheck for more than a few months. And he had a child to feed and clothe. Levi was now ten.

Still Sanders could not shake his yen for political leadership. Peter Diamondstone, one of the original Liberty Union leaders, had deep ties to the Socialist Workers Party leadership. He claims Sanders approached him in 1979 to get on the SWP ticket as the candidate for vice president. It didn't work out.

That same year Sanders joked with Sugarman about running for president as an Independent. They went as far as getting forms to get on the ballot in New Hampshire, though they never followed through. But Sugarman believed in Sanders. They often talked about politics and Sanders's prospects in the Green Mountain State. Sugarman knew Sanders was not done.

"You could say moving to Vermont was the best decision I ever made," Sanders told Mark Jacobson for *New York* magazine in 2014. "What would have happened if I'd stayed in Brooklyn? How far could I have gotten? The State Assembly?"

FIVE

THE CANDIDATE

"One person—one vote."

On Halloween night in 1980 Sanders summoned a loose-knit group of friends to the laundry room in the basement of the Franklin Square public housing project on Burlington's Old North End, a hardscrabble community near Lake Champlain where working-class families struggled to hang on.

First among them was Jim Rader, who had been Sanders's political pathfinder since Chicago. There was Richard Sugarman, the budding Jewish scholar from Buffalo who was trying to survive on an assistant professor's wages at the University of Vermont. John Franco, Chittenden County's public defender, had become a Sanders acolyte in their Liberty Union days, when Franco was a student at the University of Vermont. Dick Sartelle, a gruff-talking tenants' advocate and leader in

Burlington's low-income community, played host. "Welcome to the poor side of town," he told the gathering.

It was not a hopeful moment for Progressives. Ronald Reagan was about to be elected president. The nation was still suffering the effects of the 1973 energy crisis that exposed US dependency on Middle East oil. Islamic fanatics were holding seventy-nine American diplomats hostage in Tehran. Inflation and unemployment were high. Americans seemed to have lost faith in liberal politics after decades of big government and costly federal programs. President Jimmy Carter was a downer. The postwar boom years, FDR's expansion of big government programs, LBJ's War on Poverty—all had run their course.

Sanders chose that moment to recommit himself to his fundamental socialist beliefs. Workers were suffering. Wealthy Republicans were taking more control. Progressives had to stiffen up. "We can't abandon elective politics," he said that Halloween night. "Wishful thinking and heated discussions that make us feel good will get us only so far. We need political power."

At thirty-nine Sanders was still the face of Vermont's progressive political movement. He had dropped out of the Liberty Union Party in 1977 and quit running for office. He had stepped away from public affairs, done odd jobs, worked as a carpenter, and made a few instructional films. He had plotted a run for the White House in 1979 and gone so far as to pick up nominating petitions in New Hampshire. He still wanted to change the world. He was one of Vermont's three electors to the Socialist Workers Party convention in 1980.

"Why don't you give statewide politics a rest?" asked Sugarman. "You haven't even approached double figures, right?"

Sugarman was a philosopher capable of articulating the finer points of phenomenology, but he was also a gifted political analyst. Sharing an apartment with Sanders, Sugarman had gotten to know him during late-night sessions on life and love. In Sanders he saw a leader with special gifts, strong beliefs, and religious fervor, albeit for socialism rather than Judaism. He was the firebrand. He could stir people. He had the progressive pitch down pat. "Why don't you run for mayor of Burlington?" Sugarman suggested. "I see an opening for you."

Sugarman had analyzed the voting patterns in the 1976 gubernatorial race. Sanders had come in a distant third, but he had won 12 percent of the vote in Burlington. Most of the votes had come from working-class wards in Burlington's Old North End, home to families left out of Vermont's bucolic farming life and booming ski resorts. Many had lost manufacturing jobs when factories along Lake Champlain had changed hands or closed. "You have a natural base there," Sugarman observed.

Sanders was skeptical. He preferred a statewide or national stage. He wanted to be able to talk about the concentration of wealth and the plight of workers. But he started to see the potential—and felt the appeal to his core values. "Yeah," he said, "no one here can afford the rents now, and the rents are going up. The property taxes are high. If you live in Burlington, you should be able to work here and make a nice life for your family."

Franco agreed. A central Vermont native, he was familiar with the Democratic machine that had been running the city for decades. Mayor Gordon "Gordie" Paquette and the city council chairman would have breakfast every morning at Nectar's, a diner on Main Street, with the city's bankers and members of the longtime business families. Together they would carve up the development projects and city contracts. "That's how they run the city," Franco said.

The five friends talked through the night into the early morning. They sliced and diced the vote. They figured they could carve out a community of French speakers who lived on a peninsula that stuck out into Lake Champlain south of the city. Progressives, environmentalists, and working-class voters would join them. Sugarman vouched for the faculty at UVM. Still Sanders demurred: "Why should I run for office when I'm happily retired from politics? How could I possibly win against an entrenched political machine?"

"And," he added, "what the hell would I do if, by some miracle, I actually won?" He admitted that he had no clue about Burlington politics.

"Look," Sugarman said, "in a country where Ronald Reagan, a second-rate actor, can be elected president, why can't you be elected mayor of Burlington?"

★ ★ ★

Burlington was Vermont's Queen City, a small town on the southeastern shore of Lake Champlain. Its first mayor, Albert L. Catlin, bestowed its royal moniker in 1866.

Lovely neighborhoods lined quaint streets draped along gentle hills rolling down to the Lake Champlain shoreline. The University of Vermont and its medical center gave the city an academic appeal. Two small colleges, Champlain and Trinity, prospered nearby. Professors lived in fine homes along the hilltop avenues. Neighborhoods closer to the lakefront had an industrial feel thanks to the railroad yards and docks. The downtown was authentic but getting shabby, like a quaint house in need of renovation.

With close to 40,000 residents, Burlington was by far Vermont's largest city. The surrounding Chittenden County had about a quarter of the state's population. All of the state's major media and large industries were based in and around Burlington, including its three TV stations. Vacation homes dotted the shoreline. Ski resorts beckoned nearby. For most, life was simple and sweet.

Change came in the mid-1970s. New residents with higher expectations moved to Burlington. The universities expanded. Builders and commercial real estate brokers descended on the serene college town. A national developer proposed the state's first regional mall in Williston, just southeast of Burlington. Antigrowth groups mounted a vigorous campaign to thwart the mall, stirring Burlington awake from its slumber. The city's first urban-renewal project turned parts of downtown into a walking mall. The construction brought more stores, but it also displaced more than 200 families of a tight, ethnic neighborhood and ripped the city's downtown fabric. Speculators responded to the boom by jacking up the price of property and rents in many neighborhoods. Suddenly some families and seniors were having trouble affording their homes.

Politics in Burlington was in many ways a family affair, powered by connections and grudges in the French and Irish communities. Democrats had controlled the city's government for decades with the cooperation of the downtown business interests, lawyers, bankers, and utility company executives.

Gordie Paquette, scion of a venerable French Canadian clan, had been mayor through the 1970s. Every two years he ran for office and won easily on a platform of maintaining the status quo and not raising taxes. "A Democratic party 'machine' had been running the Queen City for most of the previous thirty years," writes Greg Guma in *The People's Republic*, his 1989 book about the city under Sanders. "Political competition, any real struggle over ideology and values, was almost nonexistent."

The status quo was not holding in 1980. Burlington was growing—painfully. Crime was up; the quality of education was down. The stately neighborhoods on the hill masked the poverty that was overtaking parts of downtown. Burlington was showing signs of urban stress.

"To make matters worse," Guma writes, "city tax revenues were no longer keeping pace with expenses, despite all the commercial growth." Rather than raise taxes to balance the $1 million shortfall, Paquette and the ruling Democrats cut services, dealing a blow to the poor and elderly. The mayor reduced budgets for parks and recreation, for fixing potholes and collecting garbage. He denigrated social programs and insisted the less fortunate would have to survive with less "handholding." He even started hinting that he might have to raise taxes.

Municipal workers took a hit. They bridled when Paquette refused to increase pay or benefits. Taking a line from Republican dogma, he declared that the city would rebound when commercial development boomed and filled the city's coffers with its taxes.

"Many people—tenants, the elderly, longtime residents of the inner city—came to believe that city hall had forgotten them," Guma explains. "Paquette became the target of their anger."

Rebuffed by the Democratic machine, activists began organizing in the community, establishing groups to advocate for tenant and welfare rights in poor neighborhoods. Block associations organized to monitor police activity, traffic, development plans, and school quality. In Burlington, finally, the times indeed were a changin'.

★ ★ ★

After the cabal's Halloween-night meeting, Sugarman dragged Sanders to the Burlington city clerk's office. They rummaged through records of election results and found the binder with the city's voting patterns in the 1976 gubernatorial campaign. There was the proof that Sanders had garnered 12 percent of the vote citywide and in Burlington's two working-class wards had carried more than 16 percent. Sanders finally relented, though he still was not convinced that running was worth the effort. He registered as an Independent, gathered the requisite number of signatures on nominating petitions, filed them with the clerk, and hit the streets.

Earlier, in October, a reporter for the *Burlington Free Press* asked Sanders whether he was pondering a run and, if so, why. Sanders responded, "The goal must be to take political power away from the handful of millionaires who currently control it through Mayor Paquette and place that power in the hands of the working people of the city who are the vast majority of the Burlington population." This reprised the standard, socialist-inspired rhetoric he had spouted since 1971. But it wouldn't wash in this municipal campaign, and he knew it. "In some ways," he writes in *Outsider in the House*, "running for statewide office was easier than running for mayor because I was more familiar with the terrain of national and statewide politics."

When he was running for governor or senator, Sanders could pepper his speeches with bromides about oppression and oligarchic control, but most Burlington residents couldn't have cared less about the alienation of the working class. They wanted clean alleys, working sewers, lower taxes, and snow cleared from their streets. The simple fact was that Sanders neither knew nor cared much about municipal affairs. He could barely find his way through all six wards. He had attended two Board of Aldermen meetings and fallen asleep at one. He found them boring. For the past decade he'd been the educator; now he needed an education.

But at least he was back in the game.

In January 1981 Democrats once again nominated Gordie Paquette to run in the March election. He acted as though his coronation were a formality. After five terms he wasn't too worried about the competition. Richard "Dickie" Bove, heir to the family that had owned Burlington's most popular Italian restaurant since 1941, announced his candidacy. Paquette's distant cousin Joe McGrath joined the race only because Gordie had pissed him off.

All it takes to win in Burlington is a simple plurality. Bove begged for votes at the bar while his father, Fiore "Babe" Bove, offered up cheap pizzas. McGrath mined disaffected Paquette kin. The incumbent barely campaigned.

"Gordie was least concerned about Sanders," says a reporter who covered the city. "Who was going to vote for a socialist?"

Paquette used Sanders as a punch line: "All Bernie wants to talk about is Vietnam and the Third World."

Sanders and his inner circle built a coalition from the streets up: they organized the activists and the advocacy groups; they roped in the environmentalists; they appealed to labor unions and teachers. Sanders forged alliances with many of these groups and promised them redress, sometimes in very specific ways. For instance, residents of Lakeside, a working-class neighborhood south of downtown, had complained for years of flooding under a bridge that literally cut them off from the rest of the city. Sanders protested with them and promised to drain the road when he was mayor.

Sanders did something he'd never had to do in statewide campaigns: he knocked on the doors of strangers and begged for their votes. How did he know which neighborhoods to hit, which buttons to push, which issues to press? John Franco was a son of the city and could provide guidance in the Irish neighborhoods, but Sanders needed help in the poorer wards. In stepped Phil Fiermonte. A native of Derby, a small town in Vermont's Northeast Kingdom, Fiermonte had graduated from the University of Vermont and stayed in the city. He applied Saul Alinsky's techniques to organizing residents of Burlington's poor neighborhoods. At the time Sanders was mounting his campaign, Fiermonte was running an organization called the King Street Area Youth Program, based in rough parts of Burlington's downtown. He had deep ties and wide contacts in the low-income community, all of which he melded into Sanders's campaign.

But Sanders didn't confine his campaign to the struggling parts of town. He made inroads to disaffected Democrats in middle-class and upscale neighborhoods too. On that front he found a crucial ally in Sadie White, a longtime member of the machine who wanted to take another route. When Paquette's downtown redevelopment forced friends and allies from their homes, she criticized the plan and broke with the party. Paquette and the Democrats ostracized her and denied her a seat in the legislature. White—feisty, elderly, and powerful— threw in with Sanders and brought her senior citizen base along.

On the political front Sanders made one brilliant move and benefited from two Paquette miscalculations. First, he borrowed a line from Reagan, telling voters, "We've been taxed enough." Paquette had called for an increase in property taxes. Sanders went out of his way to assure homeowners he would not raise their taxes, though he held the door open to raising taxes and fees on businesses. A whole new range of voters took note.

Second, he capitalized on Paquette's habit of holding down the wages of city workers, especially cops. Sanders found common ground with Joe Crepeau, president of the police union. He promised that as mayor he would meet with beat cops and bargain with the union in good faith concerning raises and benefits. The Burlington Police Patrolman's Association endorsed his bid. "Needless to say," Sanders writes in *Outsider in the House*, "their endorsement became a monumental campaign event and a major news story: a leftist populist, a former opponent of the war in Vietnam, had gained the support of the blue-collar forces of law and order!"

Burlington's Lake Champlain waterfront was a gem obscured by railroad tracks, rotting docks, and rundown warehouses. Everyone saw redevelopment of the city's lakefront as a crucial project that would determine its future: Would Burlington face the lake with parks and public access? Or would developers turn the waterfront into private property for the wealthy few?

A prominent developer and donor to Paquette's campaign had proposed building high-rise condominiums and a commercial corridor along the shore. Paquette didn't publicly support the plan, but Sanders vigorously opposed it. He envisioned parks and open space and public paths instead. "Burlington Is Not for Sale" was one of his campaign signs.

Through the frigid Vermont winter Sanders and his volunteers campaigned hard. Paquette did his best to ignore him, but Sanders demanded a debate.

The media sided with Sanders. The insurgent gave great quotes and provided regular events for WCAX, the state's major TV station, to cover in the neighborhoods. Pressure mounted on Paquette to debate his opponents until he agreed to two events. At the first he warned the audience that Sanders would wreck the city and suggested that Dickie Bove was too busy "making spaghetti" to understand the complicated matters of governing the city.

The second debate was held at the Unitarian Church on March 1, two days before the election. Paquette looked large and imperious in a gray suit. He spoke with his right hand in his pocket and gestured with his left to the audience. Sanders, dressed in a tie and jacket, had attempted to control his unruly curls and looked at the crowd through his trademark thick glasses with black frames. He was calm; Paquette was on edge. When Sanders connected the incumbent to the developer who wanted to turn the lakefront into condos and shops for the wealthy, Paquette blew. "I'm not with the big-money men," he said. "He's trying to put me with them." Looking at Sanders he predicted the Independent would turn Burlington into Brooklyn.

The audience hissed.

The *Burlington Free Press* headline the next morning read, "Sanders Picks Up More Support."

★ ★ ★

Even by Vermont standards, Election Day on March 3rd was unusually cold.

In those days before opinion polling, the best that observers could do was guess at the outcome. Sanders might get as little as 25 percent of the vote or enough to win. Paquette toured the polling places with the air of a confident incumbent. Sanders placed energetic volunteers at each one.

Bernie Sanders arose at 5:00 a.m. and hit the streets. Driving around town, he saw SANDERS FOR MAYOR posters newly tacked onto polls and being waved by volunteers. At this early date, Sanders had a decent GOTV operation. To "get out the vote," he had dispatched volunteers around Burlington to ferry low income and elderly voters to the polls. Voting was heavier than usual, perhaps by 25 percent. A big turnout was good for the challenger.

On the first count Sanders won by fourteen votes. No one in his campaign celebrated. Franco and Sugarman feared the Democratic machine would find a way to erase that slim lead, perhaps with absentee ballots. They headed for city hall.

"You'd better get in there before they steal the election," Sugarman told him.

Sanders and his lawyers demanded that the ballots be impounded and recounted. So on the night of his first victory, Sanders found himself driving down a dirt road to wake up a judge to request that the ballots be impounded. He granted the request, and the next morning the ballots were moved to the nearby state courthouse. The recount took most of the day. Franco and Sugarman kept watch.

In the recount, overseen by a judge, Sanders won by ten votes: 4,030 to 4,020. Joe McGrath, Paquette's distant cousin, got 139 votes, which proved decisive. After a decade and four lost elections Sanders had finally notched a victory.

The next morning, as news of the results spread, bankers screeched to a halt in front of Nectar's, the diner where they gathered every day to meet with the city leaders. The Paquettes vowed vengeance. The Democrats who controlled the city council agreed to make sure the Brooklyn guy would last one term at most.

"Sanders is a dead man," a Democrat told Al Gear, one of three Republicans on the council. "He won't be able to govern."

Having never had to govern anyone but himself and his

son, Sanders wondered how he would govern Vermont's largest city. At the victory party, Franco says, Sanders was hyper-
ventilating: "I had to walk him around the block. He was in
shock. Nobody took him seriously when he first announced
for mayor. He ran an asymmetric, insurgent campaign and
surprised everyone—including himself."

★ ★ ★

Jane O'Meara was working as a community organizer in Burlington's North End in 1980 when she found herself talking
about workers' rights with Mayor Paquette. "You sound like
Bernie Sanders," he told her.

"Who's he?" she wondered.

A few nights later she helped organize the mayoral debate at the Unitarian Church and found herself agreeing with
everything Sanders said. "He won me over immediately," she
admits. Along with Fiermonte, her boss at the time, she spent
the remaining days before the election canvassing and organizing for him.

Sanders had been unlucky in love. His first marriage ended
in divorce. He never married the mother of his only child. His
friends said he had given up romance for politics and raising
his son.

O'Meara could relate but had no idea how much they had
in common. She grew up in Brooklyn, not far from Sanders's
neighborhood, in a large Catholic family of diehard Democrats
devoted to JFK. He was a Bar Mitzvah; she went to Catholic school. She protested the Vietnam War while working in

Brooklyn; he wound up leading an antiwar political party in Vermont.

While O'Meara was in college in Tennessee, she married and started a family; they moved to Vermont when her husband's company transferred him to the state. She completed her college degree at Goddard and found work, first with the Burlington police and then as a community organizer. She separated from her husband in the late 1970s. The first time she saw Sanders she was divorced and raising her three children on her own.

A day after the debate Sanders breezed by her house while drumming up votes. "You've got mine," she remembers telling him, but that was the extent of the conversation. The night Sanders won the mayoral election, Fiermonte said she should come to the victory party. "I don't know anyone," she told him. "Besides, I have to take care of my kids." But he convinced her to go.

Shortly after she arrived, Sanders approached. "Wanna dance?" he asked.

For O'Meara that was it. They started to date. She joined his administration as a volunteer, creating and running the Mayor's Youth Office. She came to work dressed in blouses, suits, and skirts, quite unlike the peasant skirts and hippy garb worn by others.

Sanders and O'Meara would marry in 1988. "I couldn't ask for a better husband, father, and grandfather," she says. Sanders could not have asked for a better defender. Jane O'Meara Sanders would become a true believer of his stance on economic equality, an enforcer of his directives, and a top political advisor.

★ ★ ★

With the addition of O'Meara, Sanders had assembled the core group of insiders who would be by his side for the next forty-five years. Richard Sugarman, Jim Rader, Phil Fiermonte, John Franco, and now O'Meara would work with him, listen to him, offer their guidance, watch movies with him, accompany him to Washington, defend him, and explain him because he never wanted to waste time explaining himself.

The day after his mayoral victory Sanders held his first press conference. He chose the Franklin Square Apartments, where he had first considered the run for mayor. Dick Sartelle was by his side. Sanders seemed happy and relaxed. When reporters pressed him for details on how his progressive ideals would play out in his management of the government, he paused, then said with a slight grin, "The exciting thing is there are no models."

SIX

THE RED MAYOR

"You say you want a revolution."
—THE BEATLES

B urlington's city hall is more stolid and stately than ornate. White faux columns adorn its Georgian brick façade. Rows of eighteen-pane windows give the three floors an expansive, almost majestic look. An arch window sits atop the front entrance. When Mayor Bernie Sanders and his aides walked through the heavy door and stepped into the marble corridors on the first day of their new administration, the halls were silent, as if the place had been abandoned.

It had. The politicians and bureaucrats had abandoned ship in hopes that the new captain would quickly run aground.

If Sanders seemed surprised by his unexpected victory, Burlington's political players were apoplectic. They stewed and muttered among themselves: How could this "flatlander" and his ragtag crew of poor folks, hippies, new arrivals, disaffected Democrats, and far-left ideologues ever govern Vermont's Queen City? Vanquished Mayor Paquette was so undone that he departed immediately and spent the rest of his term on vacation. Word around Nectar's and the Ethan Allen Club, where the pillars of the city gathered, was that Sanders's victory was a "fluke" that would be duly corrected in two years. "He's the puppy that caught the car," one local politician told the *New York Times*.

Sanders knew he couldn't govern by himself. "I extend the olive branch," he told the *Burlington Free Press*. "I do not want to go to war with anybody. I don't want to fight every step of the way, and hope we'll work in cooperation."

But the cooperative spirit had died the day he was elected. Upon taking office he hired his campaign manager, Linda Niedweske, to be his secretary. The Board of Aldermen fired her. Sanders sent up the names of nominees to run the city's finance, public works, public safety, and other departments. The aldermen rejected all of his appointments in an 11–2 vote. Board president Joyce Desautels accused Sanders of trying to expand "the base of the Socialist Party in Burlington."

The FBI was curious about the socialist in charge of a small but prosperous city forty-five miles south of the Canadian line. One day after Sanders was sworn in, FBI agents showed up at the Vermont Secretary of State's Office in search of information about Sanders. Alerted to the FBI's curiosity, US District Judge Thomas Griesa a week later told a federal prosecutor, "They better do it quietly. And they better be sensitive to the fact that the mere flashing of a badge in connection with some public official . . . could get very badly misinterpreted."

Sanders didn't need any further interpretation of the aldermanic council's approach to his government. Lacking his own agency heads, Sanders called in volunteers to assemble his first budget, due that June. They sat around his dining-room table and worked the numbers with Jenny Stoler, his choice for city treasurer, and Peter Clavelle, a Burlington native who knew his way around numbers. But when Sanders submitted his budget, the council rejected it.

"We had to create a shadow government," says Peter's cousin, David Clavelle, who had worked for Senator Patrick Leahy before joining Sanders's campaign. "We had to prove we could run the government."

Sanders summoned Al Gear, one of three Republicans on the thirteen-member council. "We have to govern, right?" he asked.

"Correct," Gear said.

So Sanders offered a deal: "Give me a hand. Let's be practical and pragmatic. If you guys vote with me and we add a few Progressives, we can override the Democrats."

Gear agreed to give it a try.

Sanders sued the aldermen to establish his right to make appointments. He lost in superior court. He appealed to the state supreme court, which declined to rule on the matter. By that time it was moot. It took him nearly a year, but he finally was able to install his team in key city positions, thanks in part to the aldermanic election in 1982, which brought in a few allies and weakened his enemies. The political turn allowed him to begin advancing his agenda.

Jim Rader became city clerk and quickly used the office to procure new voting machines and restore faith in the fairness

of city elections. Sanders named John Franco assistant city attorney. Jane O'Meara, his future wife, took charge of the city's
youth council. David Clavelle, who had played a crucial role in
Sanders's campaign by showing his team how to use voter ID
to phone likely supporters, became head of civil defense. Peter
Clavelle came in to run the city personnel office.

And Richard Sugarman, the professor of religion and philosophy? "I called myself the 'minister of reality,'" he says.

Sanders still loved to discuss the broader goals of socialism:
regular folks would own the means of production, the rich would
share their wealth, and greed would evaporate. That's when the
minister of reality would weigh in. "No one gives a damn about
your ideology," Sugarman recalls telling Sanders. "The North
End wants its snow removed. The kids want nets on the hoops
in the playgrounds. Everyone wants the potholes filled."

At this early moment in his political career Sanders could
be obdurate, but he knew he needed to take advice. He started
paying attention to the practical aspects of running a northern city. During his first months in office, Burlington got a
sixteen-inch dump of heavy snow. Sanders showed up on the
streets, commiserated with his constituents, and rode shotgun
on one of the plows. The driver cleared streets in the well-to-do
neighborhoods and headed in to quit at 5:00 p.m. "Where ya
goin'?" Sanders asked.

"Day's done," the driver responded.

"Not yet," the mayor said. "How are people in the North
End gonna drive to work in the morning?" He sent the driver
back to plow the streets of the people who had elected him.

When spring finally came to Burlington—some time in

May—the mayor made sure the trash was getting picked up. He even put on work boots, grabbed a big black plastic bag, and picked up bottles and cans along one of Burlington's roads. And he made sure his trash run was covered by the media.

If picking up trash wasn't enough to endear Sanders to locals, his approach to rock concerts was. In 1979 Mayor Paquette had banned concerts in Memorial Hall. Two years later Sanders lifted the ban and encouraged rock concerts in Battery Park.

"If he didn't have the youth vote before that," says a reporter who covered him, "he nailed it with that move. Brilliant."

★ ★ ★

Once Sanders started running the city with his own team, he took control of its finances. He appointed Jonathan Leopold, a straight-up WASP bean counter, city treasurer. "Socialism is a great idea, Bernie," Leopold says he told Sanders in the early days of Burlington's progressive era. "But it just doesn't work in practice."

Leopold walked into a city financial office mired in the nineteenth century. All records and transactions were done on paper. Budget documents and city contracts were squirreled away in file cabinets. No one knew where the money was—or was going. It took him almost a year to institute a computer system to manage Burlington's budgets and procurement.

Along the way Leopold and his accountants discovered that the city had a $1.9 million surplus rather than the

$1 million deficit Paquette had projected. He found $500,000 in city funds stashed in a no-interest account when interest rates were in the double digits. He audited the city's pension fund and found that close to 100 percent of all retirees were receiving the wrong amounts. He invested the city's funds in high-interest accounts, instituted a 1 percent room and meals tax, and made utility companies pay for ripping up streets when they worked on their lines. "You don't appreciate how much free enterprise we are bringing to the city," Sanders joked to *Burlington Free Press* reporters. "Now, every moment the city's money will be at work."

The result put hundreds of thousands of dollars at Sanders's disposal. He used the funds to finance capital improvements, like sprucing up playgrounds and fixing the drainage that cut off Lakeside during major rainfalls, as he had promised during his campaign. He built new sewer and water treatment systems to stop pollution of Lake Champlain.

Sanders struck at the heart of the crony system that controlled the city's insurance business. For generations nine insurance companies had divvied up the policies. Instead Sanders put them out to bid and expected to save $200,000. Targeting developers, he raised building-permit fees for large developments and jacked up taxes for commercial properties.

One could call it good government—or redistribution of wealth. Sanders didn't qualify his style of governing, but he did build deep reserves, and he concentrated services and public works in parts of Burlington that had been neglected for decades. "One of the major priorities of the first period since I've been mayor is to take the city from what was a very inefficient government and make it into a modern corporation," he told the *Free Press* in 1982.

So much for socialism.

★ ★ ★

During his mayoral campaign Sanders rarely mentioned the "S" word. He didn't brand himself a socialist, reporters didn't press him, and Paquette, for some reason, decided not to use it as a cudgel. And when Sanders took over the city government, he never described his programs as "socialist." The "S" word faded away.

That is, until Scott MacKay, the *Burlington Free Press* city hall reporter, weighed in. Not long after the March election MacKay wrote an article detailing Sanders's socialist past and arguing that the mayor still leaned far to the left. The article burned up the wires from New York to London, and reporters descended on Burlington to inspect this unique political creature. *Rolling Stone* dubbed him "the red mayor in the Green Mountains." He was featured on Canadian and British news shows. The *Irish Evening Post*, the *New York Times*, *Newsweek*, the *Philadelphia Inquirer*, and the *Boston Globe* sent reporters to profile him.

Garry Trudeau was so intrigued he flew up to Burlington and checked out the socialist mayor over breakfast. In his July 1 *Doonesbury* comic strip, Trudeau introduced Sanders as a voice talking to *Tomorrow Show* host Tom Snyder. "I bring you greetings from the People's Republic of Burlington," the Sanders character said over a speaker, and the new name for the Queen City stuck. Readers around the nation got the joke.

The Bernie Sanders brand had blown well beyond the Green Mountains.

Burlington Democrats and Republicans had had enough of him.

A year after Sanders's first victory, *New York Times* national reporter Dudley Clendinen went to Burlington to test Sanders's continuing political prospects. Voters would have a chance to elect new aldermen in March; seven seats were up for grabs. If the Old Guard could keep its majority on the council, Sanders could be hamstrung, then tossed.

Joyce Desautels, no longer president of the Board of Aldermen, predicted that Sanders's team would win no more than one seat and that he would be gone in a year. "It'll never happen again," she said. "He's a one-term mayor."

Leo O'Connor, who wrote editorials for the *Burlington Free Press*, delivered this verdict to Clendinen: "I think that he didn't measure up to his expectations. But one thing that he probably did was to get the Democrats resolved to get their act together, and put him out."

Unfortunately for the powers that used to be, the steady obstruction of the new mayor's efforts irked many Burlington voters. In 1981 they had elected Sanders fair and square in a democratic election. Why not give him a chance to govern? With that in mind, they elected three more Progressives to the board. As soon as Sanders had additional support on the legislative side, he started campaigning for his own re-election.

The Republicans should have learned a lesson: attacking

Sanders always accrues to his benefit. But the Burlington Republicans were not quick learners. That failing would help propel Sanders to many future elections.

★ ★ ★

In his short time as mayor Sanders had demonstrated competence. Despite constant interference from the establishment, both political and financial, he and his staff had performed well, balanced the budget, found a huge surplus, plowed the snow, and avoided any major embarrassments.

To win the mayor's race in 1981 Sanders had spent a whopping $4,000. This time he raised $30,000, assembled a paid staff, ran campaign ads, and plastered the streets with posters. He ran a tight campaign and appeared headed to his second victory.

The Republicans panicked. Days before the March 1, 1983, election they took out a full-page ad in the *Burlington Free Press*. "WARNING," it blared and proceeded to list the disasters that would befall Burlington if Sanders were elected to a second term, including higher electric bills and increased unemployment. It concluded:

Mayor Sanders is an avowed socialist.

Socialist principles have not worked anywhere in the world . . . They won't work in Burlington either.

If anything, though, the negative ad boosted Sanders's fortunes. In the three-way race he won a clear majority of 52 percent of the vote. Two years later he ran for a third term

and won easily. By this time the Progressive Caucus was putting up successful candidates for aldermen, and Sanders was
working with a legislative majority. He won a fourth term in
1987 against a fusion candidate backed by both Democrats
and Republicans.

"No question, Bernie Sanders changed politics in Burlington and the entire state," says Andy Snyder, a former state legislator and state education assistant director. "He introduced
progressive politics and proved they could work."

That meant occasionally going against the progressive
grain.

In June 1983, three months after his reelection, peace
protestors started planning a demonstration at Burlington's
General Electric armaments plant. Workers at the plant were
making rapid-fire Gatling guns used by security forces in
countries such as El Salvador. Sanders was surprised when
the protest plans surfaced, and he summoned the organizers. Three came to a meeting: the writer and journalist Greg
Guma; a local activist, Robin Lloyd; and David Dellinger, a
luminary in the American radical pacifist movement who was
immortalized in Norman Mailer's *Armies of the Night* for his
prominent role in the Chicago Seven trial.

The trio told Sanders that groups had been meeting for
months to organize a peaceful protest at the GE plant. Their
planned civil disobedience would be directed not at the workers
but at the weapons, and their goal would be "plant conversion
to civilian use." Lloyd said that protesters intended to block
vehicles at the factory gate. Dellinger, then seventy-seven, said
he hoped Sanders would commiserate and at least stand down.

After all, Dellinger reminded him, the mayor had protested against the Vietnam War in Washington.

"I will have you arrested," Sanders said, according to Guma, and he accused the organizers of "blaming the workers."

On June 18 more than 500 peace activists marched through downtown Burlington demonstrating in favor of a nuclear freeze and against US intervention in Central America, among other causes. "Sanders attended," Guma wrote, "but he was sullen and uncomfortable."

Two days later, at 7:00 a.m., more than a hundred people gathered at the General Electric plant, staged a sit-in at the gate, and started blocking vehicles. From the side of the road Mayor Sanders watched as police dragged protestors away. In all, about eighty people were arrested, booked, and released. The protesters considered their action a success in disrupting business. Guma detected a change in Sanders: "Though he had gained and held on to his office through the efforts of young people, academics, activists, and neighborhood groups, he viewed his key constituencies as unions and the poor."

Sanders knew that many of his constituents would appreciate having a minor-league baseball team in Burlington. He certainly wanted one. Many of his Brooklyn buddies attest to the fact that he was forever wounded when the Dodgers decamped for Los Angeles in 1958.

Richard Sugarman told the *Sporting News* that Sanders promised to bring a minor-league franchise to Burlington during his first campaign for mayor: "He thought, correctly, that it would serve as a constructive form of recreation for the greater Burlington community." Sugarman also said Sanders preferred community ownership, along the model of Green Bay and the Packers, but that plan never materialized. Instead Sanders started negotiating with owners to bring a team to town. His efforts finally came to fruition in 1983, when the Cincinnati Reds brought their Double-A team to Burlington. The Vermont Reds played their first game on April 1, 1984.

"This is somewhat a prestigious thing to get this team," Sanders told the *Vermont Vanguard*. "I think it's going to be something the whole state can be proud of."

Word of Burlington's charm was getting out. In the 1980s travel writers started measuring the "livability" of cities, and Burlington ranked high for its climate, university and colleges, quaint downtown, and proximity to Canada, just forty-three miles to the north. The Lake Champlain waterfront finally became an inviting public space after years of controversy and false starts. Educational institutions continued to prosper, especially the University of Vermont. The city's population topped 40,000. Sanders's art councils organized jazz and blues festivals and a summer concert series that invited the Leningrad Youth Choir to sing alongside high school students from all over Vermont. Allen Ginsberg came to read poetry, Studs Terkel showed up to celebrate Workers Rights Day, and Abbie Hoffman came to town to talk about the good old hippy days, when he wrote his famous *Steal This Book*. Mayor Sanders declared June 22, 1985, "GAY PRIDE DAY" with a proclamation that noted "lesbians and gay men are making important contributions to the improvement of the quality of life in our city, state, and nation."

But Mayor Sanders was getting restless. He traveled to Nicaragua in July 1985 at the invitation of Sandinista leader Daniel Ortega. As the only elected American official at the ceremonies celebrating the sixth anniversary of the Sandinista victory over Somoza, Sanders said, "Anyone who believes the Nicaraguan nation is a military threat to the United States is obviously out of their minds." He touted Burlington's "foreign policy" and planned a trip to Cuba. Sanders married Jane O'Meara on May 28, 1988. The next day they took off for Yaroslavl in the Soviet Union, with ten others from Burlington, to complete the sister-city relationship. "Trust me," he wrote in *Outsider*. "It was a very strange honeymoon."

Says Greg Guma, "Bernie was always looking for something bigger."

★ ★ ★

The Bernie Sanders who took the microphone in 1985 after his third mayoral victory bore little resemblance to the scruffy activist shocked by his first victory in 1981. He sported a beige corduroy sport coat, a black V-neck sweater, and a white shirt that actually looked ironed. His curly hair was turning salt-and-pepper. He sat at a desk in front of a blackboard and lectured the audience of reporters and staffers. "I'm somebody who's not ashamed to say he's a radical," he began.

Before he listed his accomplishments in job creation, street improvements, and social services, he had a few words about the planet: "I want to talk about the broad question of the fate of the human race and the whole question of economic justice." He leaned over, began waving his left hand, and warned that unless elected officials and ordinary citizens discussed issues such as war and peace, "the planet may come to an end."

He promised to speak out on the "insanity of the arms race" and complained that President Reagan had proposed a $275 billion military budget while whacking away at student loans and social services. "The president is going to war not against the Soviet Union but against his own people."

Picking up the pace and raising his voice, he observed that some Americans had billions of dollars while many had none. "This requires a radical restructuring of the economy in the United States," he insisted, a refrain that would become increasingly familiar.

The mayor went on to recite his victories in public works, but he was clearly feeling constrained by municipal affairs. Burlington was too small for Bernie. If he was going to start a movement to bring about a political and economic revolution, he needed a larger audience.

All of Vermont's major television stations are based in Burlington. The dominant CBS affiliate beams news across the state, from the Canadian border down to the southern reaches. It carried images of Sanders throwing out baseballs and speaking to Kiwanis Clubs about jobs and rolling back property taxes on homes. His brand went statewide, and he took every opportunity to exploit it at the ballot box.

★ ★ ★

Dexter Randall first encountered Sanders around 1986. A Vermonter whose family goes back at least six generations, Randall was running a dairy farm near Troy, high up in the Northeast Kingdom, hard by the Canadian line. "I had 120 milking cows," he says. "I was making quite a lot of milk. I always have."

But the price of milk was dropping, and Vermont's small dairy operations were getting squeezed out. They found common cause with family farmers all over the country who were facing hard times, and their plight became a cause célèbre. Willie Nelson organized the Farm Aid concert in St. Louis to raise money for them, which in turn encouraged small farmers around the country to organize. Vermont farmers got together under the organization Rural Vermont, run at the time by Anthony Pollina.

In the fall of 1986 Rural Vermont organized a fundraiser in a town down the road from Randall's farm. He recalls a thousand farmers showing up to join forces for the sake of keeping small farms alive. And who should show up but Bernie Sanders, mayor of a big city a two-hour drive clear across the state, from the Champlain Valley to the Connecticut River Valley. "I said to myself, why is he here?" Randall recalls.

Sanders was there for a number of reasons. Pollina, who helped organize the event, was starting to advise him on farming matters. The activism of the small farmers appealed to his empathy for a working class being ground up by corporate forces. And Randall is quick to ascertain another impetus: "Undoubtedly he was trying to look beyond Burlington. He had his eyes set on something beyond the city."

Indeed Sanders had his eyes set on the governor's office.

Madeleine Kunin, a popular Democrat, was running for re-election against her lieutenant governor, Peter Smith, a Republican. Going head-to-head, Kunin would skate to a second term, but if Sanders siphoned off enough votes so that she got fewer than 50 percent, the election could be thrown to the legislature.

"We have not entered this race to win only 10 percent of the vote," Sanders said in announcing his bid for the governorship on May 12 in Montpelier, the state capital. "We are in to win." He promised to reduce property taxes and lower utility rates. "We have to have the guts to stand up to the wealthy individuals who dominate our state."

But why challenge a sitting Democrat? Sanders claimed there was little difference between Kunin and her Republican opponent. Already at odds with Vermont's Democratic Party, he told voters, "It's absolutely fair to say you are dealing with Tweedle Dum and Tweedle Dee."

Sanders's pilgrimage to Dexter Randall's farthest rural reaches of a rural state was more than a political gambit. Vermont's dairy farmers fit perfectly into his vision of working-class heroes. From his earliest days begging votes in and around the state's hills and valleys, he had equated dairy farmers with the downtrodden factory workers, farmers, and coal miners of the 1930s. Dairy farmers spent their lives milking their cows twice a day, every day; working the fields to grow hay and corn for their feed; and spreading their manure to keep the fields fertile. And for what, when the price of milk was determined by forces beyond their control?

"There were times when milk prices dropped so far down I

was all but out of money," Randall says. "I was a farmer making food, but I couldn't feed my own family."

Sanders's visit to Troy in 1986 was the first of many forays into Vermont's farmland, but a few more votes from dairymen weren't going to make him governor. Calling for class struggle, Sanders came in third with barely 15 percent of the vote. Smith doubled that with 38 percent. Kunin won with 47 percent.

One thing was certain: Sanders had severed whatever remaining ties he had to Vermont's Democrats.

★ ★ ★

Republican congressman Jim Jeffords was a well-liked Vermonter. He spoke softly but got a lot done. In 1988 he moved up to the US Senate seat that had been occupied by Bob Stafford, leaving Vermont's lone House seat open.

Sanders declared for the open seat as an Independent. Peter Smith ran on the Republican ticket; the Democratic nominee was Paul Poirier. It was Sanders's second statewide race in as many years. He lost, but he came in second, ahead of the Democrat. In fact he came darn close to beating the Republican: Sanders got 37.5 percent to Smith's 41 percent. The outcome showed Sanders and his backers that he had built a base across Vermont and could win a statewide race.

When Sanders wasn't running for office, he was adrift once again. He taught at Harvard and at Hamilton College. He considered making instructional films again, as he had a decade earlier. He contemplated his future options. "The first thing was to do what almost any sane human being would choose—drop out of politics," he writes in *Outsider in the House*, "[and] give the people of Vermont, myself, and my family a break." The second option was to run for governor again. Or he could choose option 3: try for Congress.

In 1990, when Smith was up for reelection, Sanders was lying in wait. Both declared their candidacy. The Democrats fielded Dolores Sandoval, an African American University of Vermont professor with scant political heft. Smith and Sanders would go head-to-head.

★ ★ ★

"Hi, I'm Bernie Sanders, running for Congress. If you like what's going on in Congress, then vote for Peter Smith. If not, you might want to consider voting for me."

Sanders used that line with virtually everyone he encountered on the campaign trail. Paul Teetor, who covered Sanders for the *Burlington Free Press*, called it his "Green Mountain Mantra."

Sanders, then forty-seven, hit the trail with a manic intensity, according to *Making History in Vermont*, a day-by-day account of the campaign by his press secretary, Steven Rosenfeld. The book portrays Sanders as perennially agitated, demanding, and virtually impossible to control. Considering his challenge, his demeanor might have been understandable. He was a socialist running as an Independent against a sitting congressman in a state that liked to return incumbents and had a long history of favoring Republicans. Plus Smith could raise tons of money, while Sanders's supporters were not well endowed. "I am the clear underdog in this race," Sanders liked to say.

Yet despite his fundraising prowess, Smith was not an ideal candidate. Scion of a Burlington banking family, he wasn't well known beyond Chittenden County. And he wasn't a stirring campaigner. He had the misfortune of coming off as a snooty preppie much of the time, especially in public debates and parades. And while Smith was legislating in Washington, Sanders was serving up his "Green Mountain Mantra" from Bennington to Derby, from Shelburne to White River Junction.

Sanders all but got on his knees to beg Vermont Democrats to back him. After his run against Kunin, most had no use for him, but a few—starting with Tim Corcoran, the Democratic state representative from Bennington—risked their political capital on the socialist. "There are already 100 Peter Smiths in Congress," Corcoran told the *Free Press*'s Teetor, "but there will only be one Bernie Sanders in Washington, and that will be good for Vermont. He will be noticed and he will be effective. People listen when he talks. They may not always agree, but they listen."

Sanders flew down to DC to lobby major unions for endorsements, support, and cash. The teachers union and the AFL-CIO declined. He returned to his Burlington headquarters depressed. Democrat Dolores Sandoval held a press conference calling for the legalization of drugs and accused Sanders of being "a racist" because he favored the "war on drugs," which unfairly perpetuated the stereotype that only inner-city youths had drug problems. Sanders stewed and fumed.

In July polls showed that he and Smith were deadlocked.

Sanders took his frustration out on his staff. He yelled, slammed down the phone, closeted himself, and scoffed at their advice. And he could be brusque with voters. One day he took his press secretary to lunch for a heart-to-heart talk. On the way they stopped and faced one another. "Some people say I am very hard to work with," Sanders began. "They say I can be a real son of a bitch. They say I can be nasty—I don't know how to get along with people. Well, maybe there's some truth to that." Then he proceeded to enumerate Rosenfeld's shortcomings. He told his press secretary to listen to him and do what he said, or else.

Rosenfeld stayed on through the campaign, but he now saw Sanders in a different light: "Bernie was like a parent you could never please. Nothing was ever good enough for him."

Sanders cordoned himself off with his trusted advisors— John Franco, David Clavelle, Jonathan Leopold, and Jane Sanders, whom he'd married in 1988. The candidate described them as his "family."

★ ★ ★

On the morning of January 17, 1989, Patrick Edward Purdy set his van on fire behind the Cleveland Elementary School in Stockton, California. Armed with a semiautomatic assault rifle, he positioned himself behind a building facing the playground. When the children and teachers had exited the school and gathered on the playground, Purdy started firing. He squeezed off 106 rounds in three minutes, killed five students, and wounded thirty people, including a teacher. Then he shot himself.

The bloody rampage shocked the nation.

"Why do we need assault rifles in the hands of madmen?" editorial writers asked. Congressmen tried to answer with legislation to ban assault rifles. The National Rifle Association rallied its troops and rattled its congressional allies to kill the bill.

Like any politician weaned on the mother's milk of politics—that being campaign cash—Peter Smith was well aware of the power wielded by the NRA. Already one of the most powerful special-interest groups in the nation's capital, the NRA could swing an election for or against a candidate for almost any office. Smith represented a rural state where most farm families kept a rifle or two. Vermont had no gun laws, but it did have an active NRA affiliate. Smith promised to vote against any attempt to ban assault rifles, so the NRA marked him down as a solid "No" vote. Then the congressman sat in on a hearing in which a teenage girl from DC testified about the fear she felt walking to school, knowing that there might be drug dealers packing assault rifles. Smith spoke to the student after the hearing. "That conversation had an effect on me," he says. "I changed my mind on the assault-weapons ban and decided to vote for it."

The NRA did not take the news lightly. The fact that Smith had switched his vote was worse than if he had consistently opposed them. The organization's leaders saw it as a betrayal and wanted to muscle Smith out of office, regardless of who might replace him. "Bernie Sanders is a more honorable choice for

Vermont sportsmen than Peter Smith," wrote Wayne LaPi-
erre, then and now the NRA's leader.

The Gun Owners of Vermont and local gun groups rallied against Smith. They distributed bumper stickers declaring,
"Smith and Wesson Yes; Smith and Congress No."

It's safe to assume that Sanders has rarely if ever used a
firearm. He might be able to distinguish between a revolver
and a deer rifle, but it's doubtful that he could tell the difference between a shotgun and a .22. Nevertheless in 1990 he
became a darling of the NRA, which drove thousands of gun
owners his way.

★ ★ ★

In debates Sanders drove Smith crazy with his unrelenting
attacks on Congress. He pasted Smith with a farm bill that
he said hurt family farmers. He associated Smith with cuts to
Medicare. He even tagged him with tax increases that were
part of President George H. W. Bush's budget deal.

"To me, the major issue of this campaign is a simple one,"
the challenger said at a debate before the Vermont State
Grange in Fairlee. "Do you believe the United States Congress
today represents the needs of ordinary Americans, of working
people, of the elderly? Or is it in fact a Congress significantly
bought and sold by large corporations and wealthy individuals
who are using that Congress for their own personal gain rather
than for the needs of all of the people? That is the fundamental
issue."

Smith pursed his lips, peered at Sanders, and responded:
"For twenty years he's been walking around Vermont saying,

'Tax the wealthy.' And then he has a chance to actually do it, what does he do? He goes for the back door."

Smith might have had a point, but he made no headway with the farmers, who warmly applauded Sanders.

★ ★ ★

On October 23, two weeks before Election Day, *Air Force One* touched down at Burlington International Airport and delivered President Bush for a quick stop in the Queen City. It was the first of three presidential stops in New England to support candidates on the brink, like Peter Smith.

The president was scheduled to attend a pancake-and-apple breakfast at the Sheraton Conference Center for 700 GOP loyalists, who would fork over $125 each to dine with the commander in chief. For $500 more, a fan could have a picture taken with the president.

The day before, Sanders had recorded a radio ad welcoming Bush: "My hope is that when President Bush comes to Vermont tomorrow, he could do something more than just raise $500 a plate for my Republican opponent, Mr. Smith. It would, I think, be very good for him to go out in the street and talk to the elderly and tell why he thinks it's necessary to slash Medicare, talk to workers and tell them why he thinks it's necessary to raise gas taxes. Maybe he could learn from coming to Vermont and doing the right thing."

Smith offered the president an even more biting welcome. Standing up next to Bush, who was seated at the Sheraton's long head table, he started his speech by criticizing Bush's veto of the 1990 Civil Rights Act the week before. Bush stopped eating, wiped his mouth, and turned toward his critic. If Bush thought his New England trip would provide a respite from nasty budget battles and the ridicule he'd faced after reneging on his "No new taxes" pledge, Smith had other objectives.

"Ask yourselves," Smith said, "why did this president, last May, decide that the issue he had run on and won on had to be laid on the table as a point of negotiations? We're talking about his pledge on taxes. He did it because he understood that the good of this country had to come first." Smith wasn't against the taxes; he just wanted to drive home the president's hypocrisy.

Smith wasn't done boxing the president's ears. He mentioned his "specific disagreements" with Bush, then played the president as a pawn in his conflict with Sanders: "And let me tell you, Mr. President, I believe the people of Vermont are ready and willing to support higher tax brackets on the wealthy as an important part of any package to get this country out of deficit spending."

Even Smith wanted to "eat the rich."

More tightlipped than usual, the president then stood, gave Smith a backhanded compliment as "a man of independent mind," and spoke for thirty minutes on national security and domestic spending. He lingered for another half hour, then flew off to New Hampshire. Trashing the president didn't boost Smith's prospects on either end. In Washington his remarks came off as an inhospitable betrayal; Vermonters scowled at his disrespectful treatment of a president who had flown up to show support for a one-term congressman.

Adding to Smith's misery, the NRA had mailed "Dump

Smith" letters to Vermont's 12,000 members and started running anti-Smith radio ads.

As he continued to slide in the polls he resorted to a tactic that always helped Sanders: he went negative.

With a heavy media buy, Smith ran a TV advertisement accusing Sanders of saying he had been "physically nauseated" by JFK's soaring "Ask not" inaugural address and of praising Fidel Castro while criticizing congressional Democrats. It concluded, "Those are not Vermont values, Bernie. Keep Vermont proud. Keep Peter Smith in Congress."

But Smith's gambit backfired. Reporters dissected the ads and found that he had taken Sanders's quotes out of context. The *Rutland Herald* compared Smith to the red-baiting congressman Joe McCarthy. The *Burlington Free Press*, which had endorsed Smith, urged him to take down the ads.

Rather than replying in kind, Sanders donned his gray tweed jacket and made a final ad in which he sat calmly in a library and listed the "enormous challenges" facing the country, including the growing gap between rich and poor, pollution, and rising health care costs. "The list is a long one, and it saddens me that my opponent, finding himself behind in the polls, is now resorting to the most negative and dishonest advertising this state has ever seen. I don't think that's the way to run a campaign, and I think most Vermonters agree with me." He paused and looked deeply into the camera. "I've run a positive and honest campaign," he concluded, "and that's the way I'll represent you in Congress."

★ ★ ★

November 6 dawned dark and rainy, but the grim weather passed and voters turned out in large numbers. The polls closed at 7:30 that night, and the results started spilling out half an hour later. Early tallies showed Sanders with a nearly 20 percent lead. It fell as low as 10 percent, but he seemed to be trouncing Smith in every county.

When it appeared that Sanders had prevailed, but before the final results were in, he showed up at his victory party, where hundreds of his supporters had already gathered. He told them, "Things look good," and promised to return. At 10:15 he took the podium.

"As I understand it, Congressman Smith has just conceded," he announced. The crowd responded with chants of "Bernie! Bernie!" He raised his hands, then lowered them to calm the crowd. Then he spoke. And spoke. He praised his staff and volunteers and said, "I am as proud as I can be of the people in our state, who showed the courage to go outside the two-party system. Showed the courage to stand up to the president and the vice president and every multinational corporation in America."

Later he reminded the gathering that he alone couldn't bring about change: "What we need in this country is a mass movement of tens of millions of people who are prepared to stand up and say: 'We want national health care!'"

The applause and yells drowned him out.

"We want the millionaires and the multinational corporations, who have not been paying their fair share of taxes, to start paying."

The crowd cheered.

"We want the money going into education, environmental protection."

More cheers.

Finally Sanders called for Vermonters to take the lead in a political revolution—"a political revolution which TAKES POWER AWAY from the multinationals and the wealthy and gives it back to the people, where it BELONGS!"

Somewhere in the crowd a man yelled, "We love you, Bernie!"

SEVEN

THE LONER

"Do I think there are people who will dislike me in Congress because of my style and because of my views? I do."
—BERNIE SANDERS, 1997

On August 2, 1990, Saddam Hussein's Republican Guard forces invaded Kuwait, a small nation along Iraq's southern border. When Saddam was an ally, America had outfitted him with tanks and planes. Now an enemy tyrant, he used those arms to sweep into the weaker Persian Gulf nation and set its oil fields aflame. He had been threatening war, but his attack still caught the United States off guard.

A week later President George H. W. Bush sent troops to Saudi Arabia to forestall further Iraqi aggression. But that was not enough. The president wanted to bring the full force of the US military to bear on the Iraqi aggressors. Declaring war required congressional authority. He would seek it in

January 1991, weeks after rookie Vermont congressman Bernard Sanders took office.

To say Sanders was unprepared for Washington and life as a congressman is an understatement. His too short khaki pants and tweed jacket made him look like a staffer in the halls of the US House of Representatives. He and Jane were short of cash, but they bought him a few gray suits. They rented a place a few blocks from the House office buildings, but finding it too big and expensive they soon traded down to a basement efficiency in a house owned by another congressman.

As part of the orientation for new congressmen, the president invited Bernie and Jane to the White House. It was a cordial affair, of course, and the Bushes greeted the newcomers warmly. At one point First Lady Barbara Bush took Jane by the elbow and chatted with her for a while. Both Sanderses recalled her saying, "Your husband defeated that man who was so rude to the president. Welcome to Washington. Let me know if I can help you in any way."

The graciousness did not extend to politics and the impending vote on the Persian Gulf War.

Sanders joined California congressman Ron Dellums and others in an ad hoc antiwar caucus working to prevent full hostilities, and he traveled back to Montpelier to attend an antiwar demonstration. Having begun his political activism by protesting the Vietnam War, he was primed to oppose sending troops to the Middle East for what he considered a war to protect the US oil cartel.

Sanders took to the House floor days before the congressional vote. He acknowledged that Saddam was "an evil person" and that his actions in attacking Kuwait were "illegal,

immoral, and brutal." "It seems to me, however, that the challenge of our time is not simply to begin a war which will result
in the deaths of tens of thousands of people, young Americans,
innocent women and children in Iraq, but the real challenge
of our time is to see how we can stop aggression, how we can
stop evil in a new way, in a nonviolent way."

In one of his first speeches in the well of the House chamber, he kept pressing for nonviolent solutions. "If we are not
successful now," he asserted with prescience, "then I think all
that this world has to look forward to in the future for our
children is war, and more war, and more war."

The House voted 250 to 183 to approve Bush's plan for
full hostilities.

Two days later CNN's correspondent Peter Arnett reported
from Baghdad that US planes had begun bombing parts of the
Iraqi capital. It was the start of Operation Desert Storm, an
American-led, multilateral show of force that would compel
Saddam to withdraw his troops from Kuwait. President Bush
exulted, and most Americans rejoiced. The day after the bombs
began to fall, Congressman Sanders took to the House floor
once again and delivered a guns-or-butter polemic, arguing
that the cost of war would hurt the homeless and rob Americans of hopes for the kind of "national health care system"
enjoyed by people in most other countries of the industrialized
world. "I predict this Congress will soon be asked for more
money for bombs, but there will be no money available to re-
industrialize our nation so that our working people can have
decent-paying jobs. There will be no money for education and
for our children—twenty-five percent of whom live in poverty.
There will be no money available for the environment or to

help the family farmer—many of whom are being forced off the land today in my state of Vermont and throughout this country." He warned too of cuts in Medicare and Social Security to pay for the war.

It sounded in many ways like the left-wing version of the fearmongering diatribe that hawks might deliver about the impending onslaught of Soviet missiles unless the United States developed more nuclear warheads. Sanders's antiwar rhetoric was heartfelt, but it was to little avail. Republicans drafted—and in March the House approved—a resolution supporting the commitment of troops to the region, with an amendment commending Bush for his decisive leadership, unerring judgment, and sound decisions in making war. "I was incredulous," Sanders wrote in *Outsider in the House*; to him the measure sounded "like some Stalinist propaganda of the 1930s."

On the day of the vote Sanders slipped his card into the machine that tallies votes and pushed "No"—one of only six members who voted against the resolution; 399 voted yes. When the count was announced, Sanders thought to himself, "This is going to be a short congressional career."

He felt lonely in Washington—and worse back home in Vermont. When he returned to see a unit of the Vermont National Guard off to the Persian Gulf, he was greeted by boos. Waiting for a flight to Washington one day at the Burlington airport, he was confronted by a woman who said, "My son is over there. I'm appalled that you're not supporting him."

Sanders sputtered. She turned and walked away.

★ ★ ★

The new congressman and his wife were so broke after his election that they had to borrow money from friends for a brief trip to Mexico before settling into their new lives. When they returned, Progressives threw a "Welcome to DC" party for them at Eastern Market on Capitol Hill. Jesse Jackson and Ralph Nader were among the liberal luminaries who said they expected big things from Sanders.

He was, after all, only the fourth avowed leftist elected to Congress in the twentieth century—and the first since 1950. In the early 1900s New York City elected Meyer London and Milwaukee sent Victor Berger to Congress; both were Socialist Party members. Vito Marcantonio ran on the American Labor Party ticket in the 1930s and represented New York City off and on until his defeat in 1950.

Steven Soifer wrote in *The Socialist Mayor* that Sanders went to Congress on a wave of populist appeal: "For the first time in decades class issues were once again part of the US mainstream political discourse." Soifer predicted a "political backlash" from the excesses of the Reagan years. "Taxing the rich became a popular theme in Washington, pitting the party of the rich against the party of low- and moderate-income people."

Soifer's estimations turned out to be largely wishful thinking. If there was a progressive moment, it was fleeting. President Bush's Persian Gulf War turned out to be a win in the public's mind. The 1994 elections saw the ascension of conservative Republicans, who drove dozens of Democrats out of office and took control of the House. Newt Gingrich became speaker and issued his "Contract for America," which called for lower taxes and smaller government. "I disagree with everything Gingrich stands for," Sanders wrote in *Outsider in the House*, "but I was impressed by the scope of his vision. He thinks big." Democrat Bill Clinton succeeded Bush and was president for two terms, but his brand of governing was much more centrist than leftist and often not progressive enough for Sanders.

Meanwhile the National Rifle Association began exercising inordinate power in Washington. The NRA had helped Sanders defeat Peter Smith in 1990, but it turned against him in 1992, when it printed "Bye Bye Bernie" bumper stickers. Sanders found himself navigating between gun owners in Vermont and liberals who expected him to battle for gun control. He enraged many of his supporters when he voted again and again against versions of the Brady Bill, which mandated background checks and waiting periods for gun purchases from licensed firearms dealers. "Those early days in Congress were very tough," he admitted in his memoir.

★ ★ ★

Sanders acted as though he had been dropped behind enemy lines. "This place is not working," he told Vermont's Associated Press bureau chief, Chris Graff, in September 1991, after eight months in office. "It is failing. Change is not going to take place until many hundreds of these people are thrown out of their offices."

With a dose of bravado he continued, "What you see, on major issue after major issue, is that the Congress does not have the courage to stand up to the powerful interests. I have the freedom to speak my mind and, ultimately, right now in

American politics, we need to raise the issues these guys don't want to, and I can do that."

Criticizing Congress and Washington had become a winning strategy after Reagan took that route to the White House in 1980. It was, of course, the height of hypocrisy in all but a few cases. Incumbents—who, by definition, were denizens of the political capital—ran against Washington even though they were part of it. Newcomers ran hard against Washington, then, once elected, changed course and joined the club, strutting around in pinstripe suits, raising gobs of campaign cash, and bending their ideals to suit the winds.

Not Bernie Sanders. The Vermont socialist genuinely disliked Congress.

"I'm not an insider," he told a *New York Times* reporter in Vermont right after his election. "I know who I am." Between bites of a McDonald's pastry, he added, "I know where I came from. I don't need to get down on my knees and ask rich people for their help. The point of this is to show the nation that we, here in Vermont, have given people a real political alternative."

As for DC, he told UVM professor Garrison Nelson in 1992, people "have no idea how totally corrupt it is," according to a 2015 article in the *New Yorker*. He told other reporters back then, "If I ticked off five or six issues from my campaign, there's no way Congress can deal with them. It's totally out of touch."

In turn, Sanders's colleagues were not thrilled to have him in their midst, running them down at every turn. House Democrats refused to give him a spot in their caucus unless he abandoned his Independent status and joined the party. "I am an Independent," he told Vermont reporters, "and I intend to remain an Independent." The Democrats seated him on less-than-powerful committees, but he called his assignments victories nonetheless.

When Congress actually functions, it does so largely on the basis of collegiality, compromise, and camaraderie. Sanders had no time for any of that. He railed on the House floor, scoffed at legislation he considered beneath him, and ignored offers of collaboration.

Joe Moakley, a liberal Democrat from Massachusetts, would have made a natural ally. Instead Sanders was "out there wailing on his own," Moakley said. Barney Frank was one of the few congressmen who bothered to endorse Sanders when he challenged Smith in 1990. Having come out as one of the first gay congressmen, Frank was not afraid of bucking the tide or standing up for principle. "Bernie alienates his natural allies," Frank said after defending Sanders during his first term. "His holier-than-thou attitude, saying in a very loud voice he is smarter that everyone else and purer than everyone else, really undercuts his effectiveness."

Vermont's two senators, Democrat Patrick Leahy and Republican James Jeffords, took that into account when they learned that Sanders had been invited to a meeting with Agriculture Secretary Edward Madigan about falling milk prices. "Why even go now?" one of the senators asked rhetorically, according to a *Washington Post* article. "We knew Bernie will start yelling and screaming." An aide said his senator was not happy that Sanders would be at the meeting because "Bernie had been publicly bad-mouthing the administration non-stop. It would not have been a conducive environment for negotiation."

Jeffords ran into Sanders at a political reception and un-invited Vermont's lone congressman from the meeting, which could have proved crucial to Vermont farmers. Apparently Sanders was not miffed. He told *Washington Post* reporter Lois Romano, "If someone says, 'Look, Bernie, we are all getting together and we want to compromise and cut a deal,' and I say 'I don't want to compromise,' I can understand why they don't want me there." He explained his situation to another journalist this way:

> Let me be frank. Do I think there are people who will dislike me in the Congress because of my style and be-cause of my views? I do. I did not come here to be one of the nicest guys or be elected the most pleasant member of Congress. The people of Vermont did not send me down here to get patted on the back. If there are some people who don't like me, there's nothing I can do about it . . . But I hope people don't confuse bluntness with rudeness. Too many times around here people say: "My honorable good friend, colleague this and that." I say, "Okay, c'mon, let's get to the issues."

Even as he found himself derided and excluded, Sand-ers was growing more comfortable in his role. He even found some like-minded legislators and started the Congressional Progressive Caucus in 1991 with six members, including Or-egon's Peter DeFazio; Lane Evans, a Vietnam veteran from Illinois; and Maxine Waters of California. It has gradually grown to seventy-five members organized around Sanders's fundamental issues: preserving Social Security and Medicare, advocating for alternative forms of energy, job creation, and a host of liberal, lefty causes.

Meanwhile Sanders managed to see his life in simple terms. "I work in Washington," he wrote. "I live in Vermont."

★ ★ ★

In the spring of 1991 Dexter Randall was one hay bale away from bankruptcy. He was still milking 120 or so cows, but the price of milk was so low he couldn't make ends meet. He wasn't the only family farmer in Vermont's Northeast Kingdom who was suffering that April. Randall helped organize a protest at the Agri-Mark milk-processing plant near St. Johnsbury. The farmers maneuvered their tractors into a circle around the plant. Congressman Sanders showed up to provide support.

"Bernie got up and spoke," Randall recalls. "He was always there for the family farmers. He was always looking out for our best interests."

Randall, whose forebears settled in nearby Lyndon around 1795, spoke about the falling milk prices and price-gouging practices that he alleged were making the milk processors rich and keeping the farmers poor. The family farmers fit perfectly into Sanders's class-warfare economic calculus. The irony was this: Vermont's senators didn't trust him to not screw up a meeting about milk prices in Washington, but he could make Vermont farmers believe he was all but at their side in the milking parlor.

"Over the years I have developed an almost emotional attachment to the state's dairy farmers," he wrote in *Outsider in the House*, "and have fought hard for them against overwhelming odds." He acknowledges that he did not know one end of a cow from the other when he arrived in Vermont. But by 1991 he had forged strong ties with farmers across the state, thanks in part to Randall; Anthony Pollina, a member of his staff and a future state legislator; and Jennifer Nelson, a dairy farmer from Rochester who also joined Sanders's Vermont staff.

Despite the protests and the speeches, Randall still couldn't feed his wife and five children. So he swallowed his pride and drove to Newport, a town about twenty miles east, at the southern end of Lake Memphremagog, which straddles the Canadian border. He walked into the social services office and applied for food stamps. "They threw me out," he says. "There was a rule about farmers not being eligible for food stamps."

Randall says Sanders got word of his travails and interceded, so "farmers like me could feed their families." The farming community learned that Congressman Sanders was on their side, so when Randall organized a pig roast for Sanders the following September, his field filled up with pickup trucks, farmers, and their families. In a relatively barren corner of the Green Mountain State, a crowd of 300 is what Sanders would call a "yooooge" gathering. "They came out of the woodwork to see Bernie," Randall says. "All walks of life showed up in that field. They could relate to his message about taking care of the land and the people—basic pocketbook issues, loud and clear, every time."

Sanders went home to Vermont nearly every weekend, making stops at town hall meetings, parades, county fairs, and random farmhouses. Pollina tells of driving Sanders on Vermont's back roads, when the congressman might tell him to pull off between a barn and a farmhouse so he could see if anyone was home and have a cup of coffee.

"If there are 600,000 people in the state of Vermont, Bernie has probably stood beside and touched 300,000 of them," says former state legislator Andy Snyder. "And he's probably fed them too." Sanders often provided spaghetti or lasagna dinners at his town hall meetings.

Call it what you will—a Sanderista cult, a brand, a following—Vermonters responded to Sanders. They got his quirkiness, his occasional irascibility, his deep love of Vermont and of them. They appreciated his dedication to their interests—that is, when he had time between skirmishes in his perpetual class warfare.

Sanders had to test his constituents' devotion every two years, and each time his enemies tried to knock him off.

★ ★ ★

Republicans and the political establishment called Sanders's 1990 victory "a fluke," just as they had his first mayoral win a decade before. But then he won again in 1992 and 1994. By 1996 they had had enough of the freak socialist, who was sticking around and starting to make headway in the legislative process.

Take the minimum wage. Sanders introduced a bill in 1993 to raise the minimum wage to $5.50 an hour and index it to inflation. The US Chamber of Commerce, the National Federation of Independent Businesses, and the National Association of Manufacturers lined up against the bill. Sanders pointed out that countless corporate executives and their lobbyists were pulling down millions of dollars a year, yet they couldn't bear to see a worker who was making $8,840 get an increase of $2,000. The bill made it to the House floor.

He got an audience with President Clinton, who was sympathetic but opposed the minimum-wage increase because it detracted from his push for health care reform. Sanders's bill died. But in 1996 the Democratic leadership got behind another bill to increase the minimum wage. House leaders paraded low-wage workers through press conferences. Senator Ted Kennedy lobbied hard for the bill. It passed by a vote of 354 to 72.

Although it wasn't Sanders's legislation, many corporate leaders blamed him for it. They had yet another reason to want him out of Congress when he successfully added an amendment to the 1995 Defense Appropriations Bill eliminating $31 million in bonuses for executives at defense contractor Lockheed-Martin; the bonuses were billed as "restructuring costs" for eliminating as many as 17,000 jobs. "Payoffs for lay-offs," a Sanders's aide called the provision as the congressman killed it.

This was war.

The Republican National Committee, at the behest of many large corporate donors, put an "X" on Sanders in the 1996 election cycle. They targeted his seat and contributed heavily to his opponent, Susan Sweetser, a popular young Vermont state senator considered a rising star among Vermont Republicans. Lockheed-Martin maxed out with a $10,000 contribution to her campaign. Republican majority leader Dick Armey showed up in Vermont to campaign for her, as did GOP presidential candidate Steve Forbes and House

Budget Committee chairman John Kasich. "They wanted me out, badly," Sanders wrote.

On May 27, 1996, a lovely spring day in Burlington, Sanders announced his reelection bid before 150 supporters. To pump up the crowd he'd lined up an impressive group of speakers, ranging from union bosses to disabled veterans to Peter Clavelle, his mayoral aide who had followed him as mayor.

Jacket off and shirtsleeves rolled up, his white hair tousled by the wind, Sanders talked of standing up to "a Republican president when he was wrong and a Democratic president when he was wrong . . . a Democratically controlled Congress when they were wrong and a Republican-controlled Congress when they were wrong. . . . And that's what I have done."

Fifteen years before the Occupy Wall Street movement popularized the notion that wealth was concentrated among 1 percent of Americans, Sanders was making the case:

> During the 1980s, the top 1 percent of wealth holders in this country enjoyed two-thirds of all increases in financial wealth. The bottom 80 percent ended up with less real financial wealth in 1989 than in 1983—and that trend continues. Today—tragically—the United States has the most unfair distribution of wealth and income in the entire industrialized world.
>
> Justice, an economy in which all people do well, not just the very rich, is what I've been fighting for.

He excoriated Gingrich, Armey, and their Republican allies for their efforts to gut social programs and aid to veterans while raining tax breaks on the wealthy and financing "Star Wars gadgets that the Pentagon doesn't want."

Then he hit the campaign trail, just as he had nearly every two years for the past quarter of a century. This time—for the first time—he hired a political consultant, Democratic strategist Tad Devine. Sanders worked hard to raise $1 million— far more than he'd ever taken in—because he knew Sweetser would have almost unlimited campaign funds. Indeed the RNC kicked in $123,600, the maximum allowed by law. Armey raised $30,000 for Sweetser, Kasich $25,000, and New York's GOP representative Bill Paxon $40,000. An independent expenditure committee pumped in tens of thousands more. "We're going to pull out all the stops [to bring down] that god-awful Bernie Sanders," said Paxon, who was chairman of the Republican Congressional Campaign Committee. The NRA rallied its members with robocalls demanding Sanders's defeat.

Sanders countered with comedian Al Franken, years before he became a US senator from Minnesota. Television entertainer Bill Maher had Sanders on his show; progressive filmmaker Michael Moore raised funds for him in Burlington; Gloria Steinem pitched in with a rally at the University of Vermont.

Neither the names nor the money on either side seemed to make much of a difference. Bernie was a brand, and Vermonters had come to adore him. He was electorally impregnable. A bit more than a month before the election he was ahead by 15 to 20 points in a variety of polls.

At that point Sweetser got desperate and made the mistake that has sunk many would-be Sanders slayers: she tried to go beyond negative to downright dirty. She hired Cathy Riggs—a private investigator, GOP operative, and wife of right-wing California congressman Frank Riggs—to dig up any slime she could find on Sanders. Riggs called Deborah Messing, who'd been married briefly to Sanders right out of college. Rather than spilling, Messing hung up the phone and called her friend Anthony Pollina, who got in touch with Sanders, who then talked with Messing. Having gone to the source and confirmed Riggs's sordid efforts, Sanders called in the reporters.

AP bureau chief Chris Graff interviewed Riggs, who said, "I'm very thorough. I do a total, complete package. Contacting the ex-wife is just something on my checklist." Graff wrote, "But clearly it is not on the checklist of Vermonters. Riggs's call to Sanders's ex-wife was viewed in Vermont as crossing the line. It's not fair play. It's not Vermont-like."

At first Sweetser's campaign denied the incident, calling it "innuendo and hearsay." That lasted until Messing reluctantly stepped forward and confirmed the call.

A week before the election, one poll showed Sanders's lead at 13 percent, a margin that held up through Election Day, when he polled 140,678 votes to Sweetser's 83,021.

It might have been his last tough race on Capitol Hill.

★ ★ ★

Each victory in Vermont emboldened Sanders in Washington. He appointed himself the bulwark against Gingrich's "greed and bigotry and scapegoating." Using his position as chairman of the Congressional Progressive Caucus, he helped put forward alternative budgets proposing increased spending on social programs. Every year he submitted legislation to establish a single-payer health care system. He tried to increase the minimum wage. Few of his major efforts met with success, but Sanders was able to write and pass other measures. The first was the National Cancer Registries Act, which created a system of uniform statistics on every case of cancer. He successfully blocked attempts to gut federal aid for winter home-heating programs. He railed against the Defense of Marriage Act, which defined marriage as the union of one man and one woman. Congress passed the bill, which was law until the Supreme Court ruled it unconstitutional in 2015.

Sanders added to his progressive credentials when he took on the pharmaceutical industry for gouging Americans with high-priced drugs. Vermonters often appealed to him to help them find a way to reduce the cost of their medicines. In 1999 Sanders took a busload of seniors across the Canadian line so they could purchase medicine at a lower cost. He became the first congressman to take constituents to Canada to prove his point that drug companies were taking advantage of Americans.

On military matters, however, Sanders could occasionally come off as a baby hawk, if not a full-fledged warmonger. After voting against sending troops to Iraq in 1990, he consistently voted to fund the war. In April 1999 he voted for the NATO bombing of Yugoslavia. This vote pushed some Vermont progressives over the edge. Members of Sanders's former party, Liberty Union, organized an "Instant Antiwar Action Group." Twenty-five Vermonters occupied Sanders's Burlington office; police arrested fifteen.

"Bernie's selling out says clearly to working people and those unable to find work that even leftists become mainstream politicians," wrote Will Miller in the Liberty Union's newsletter, "when and if they win office." Sanders did not comment on the sit-in. He was in Washington, DC, at the time and missed the protest. It didn't faze him.

Having grown more comfortable in the House, Sanders got antsy and looked for his next political challenge. In 2000 word was that he intended to take on incumbent Republican senator Jim Jeffords, a popular moderate. Sanders demurred but did use the moment to move up. Speaker Dick Gephardt urged Sanders to remain in the House to help maintain the fragile Democratic majority. Though an Independent, Sanders voted nearly 90 percent of the time with Democrats. Sanders said he would stay in the lower chamber, but in return he wanted a spot on the powerful Appropriations Committee. Gephardt delivered.

"The conventional wisdom is that a senator is more powerful than a congressman," Jane Sanders told a Vermont reporter. "But if you're an appropriator, it kind of evens things up."

Sanders "evened things up" with the NRA in 2005, when he voted for the Protection of Lawful Commerce Act. Written by and for the NRA and other gun rights groups, the bill gave gun manufacturers the kind of protection from lawsuits that other industries could only dream of: it protected gun makers and gun dealers from being sued if guns they sold were later used in crimes, unless they "knowingly" sold them to straw buyers. There was no reason to support this bill other than to exhibit blatant support for the gun industry. Sanders always explained away his gun rights votes by telling critics that because Vermont was a rural state, most of his constituents had rifles in their closet. But that was no reason to provide legal shelter for gun manufacturers that no other industry enjoys.

On the Appropriations Committee Sanders was able to steer funds to Vermont and other favorite projects. And he could make his voice heard regarding major economic matters when, for instance, Federal Reserve chair Alan Greenspan appeared before the House Committee on Financial Services in July 2003. "I have long been concerned that you are way out of touch with the needs of the middle class and working families in our country," he told Greenspan. "And I must tell you, your testimony today only confirms all of my suspicions."

When Greenspan dismissed Sanders's concerns that America was losing jobs to companies abroad, Sanders retorted, "Today you reached a new low, I think, by suggesting that manufacturing in America doesn't matter."

Greenspan responded, "The incomes, the purchasing power, are far more important than what it is we produce."

To which Sanders replied, "That is an incredible answer."

Incredible in its own right was the fact that Sanders declined to lecture Greenspan further and left it at that.

EIGHT

THE SOCIALIST SENATOR

"It's been a pleasure to do combat with him."
—Senator John McCain, 2014

From a distance Bernie Sanders's announcement in 2005 that he was running for Vermont's open seat in the US Senate seemed preposterous. He was a sixty-four-year-old Independent who thought he could become the first socialist elected to the most powerful legislative body in the world. "Liberal" was still a dirty word. Slim chance.

But from the vantage point of the Green Mountains, Sanders was a fan favorite. "Bernie," as Vermonters called him, was the natural successor to Senator Jim Jeffords, who was retiring after three terms. Vermonters loved Jeffords, a quiet, unassuming gentleman best known for switching from Republican to Independent in 2001 to protest the rightward drift of the GOP. In one bold move he had denied Republicans

control of the Senate. Like Jeffords, Sanders suited Vermonters' preference for iconoclasts. Sanders would run on the same
platform Vermonters knew so well because his priorities had
not changed since 1980, when he'd run for mayor of Burlington: rights of workers, aid for the vanishing middle class, national health care, closing the large gap between rich and poor,
changing a disastrous trade policy.

"My major emphasis will be on economic issues," he told
In These Times in May 2005, and "bringing about a fundamental political change in this country" led by the "grassroots."

Was Sanders afraid he would be red-baited?

"Afraid of being red-baited?" he asked incredulously. "I'm
being red-baited already. Everybody in Vermont knows that
I'm a democratic socialist. It's so well known that nobody
talks about it anymore. But suddenly, now all over the national
media, it's 'socialist, socialist, socialist.' Of course, the Republicans and the corporate media are going to red-bait me."

If Sanders wasn't worried about being called out as a
socialist, neither did he seem all that concerned about his
seemingly formidable Republican opponent, Richard Tarrant.
Tarrant was a candidate out of central casting. In myriad ways
he was the anti-Sanders. Tarrant was tall and ramrod straight;
Sanders walked with a slight stoop. Tarrant's hair was thick
and silvery; Sanders's was white, wispy, and thinning. Tarrant strode the world with a chin-forward, hail-fellow-well-
met smile; Sanders frowned his way through the day. Tarrant
looked like a US senator; Sanders still came off as a college
professor. Tarrant was a businessman who had made a fortune
in the health technology field; Sanders had never worked in
the private sector and had accumulated only modest savings.

Like Sanders, Tarrant had not been born in Vermont. But Tarrant had a Florida problem: while building his business in Vermont, he had been building a mansion and paying property taxes in Florida. Vermonters took issue with his dual residency. Unlike Tarrant, Sanders had something no amount of good looks and cash could overcome: he had earned the respect, if not the political love, of the great majority of Vermont voters.

The two very different candidates waged a spirited campaign. Tarrant plunked down more than $7 million of his own money to knock Sanders off. Sanders raised $6.5 million to ensure his move from the House to the Senate. Both filled the airwaves with political ads, but Tarrant made the mistake of going negative. He misrepresented Sanders's voting record to make it seem as if he had opposed a bill raising the minimum wage and another protecting exploited and missing children. In fact the first included tax breaks for wealthy Americans, which Sanders refused to endorse; the second bill was unconstitutional.

"If Bernie Sanders is elected," Tarrant said in an interview during the campaign, "not a single business will move to Vermont. Period. I know this firsthand."

The candidates engaged in thirteen public debates. Looking senatorial, Tarrant trumpeted his success in bringing jobs to Vermont and called Sanders "the best problem pointer-outer" for repeating his litany of wrongs against the working class, economic inequality, and the excesses of the rich. But Vermonters didn't seem to mind.

Democratic leaders were so convinced that Sanders could demolish any challenger that they didn't even nominate a candidate. Besides, New York's senator Chuck Schumer, chair of the Democratic Senatorial Campaign Committee, supported Sanders, which meant that no Democrat could expect cash from the committee. By coincidence Schumer was a Brooklyn native who had graduated from James Madison High, Sanders's alma mater. So it was Republican versus Independent all the way.

When the votes were counted, Sanders had trounced Tarrant, who managed to pull in just 33 percent. At more than $12 million, the race was by far the most costly campaign ever in Vermont. Tarrant wound up spending roughly $100 for each vote he received.

Beyond Vermont the media seemed obsessed about Sanders's political leanings. A *Washington Post* reporter asked if he accepted his notoriety for being the only socialist ever to serve in the Senate. "Yeah," he said, "I wouldn't deny it. Not for one second. I'm a democratic socialist. In Norway, parents get a paid year to care for infants. Finland and Sweden have national health care, free college, affordable housing, and a higher standard of living. Why shouldn't that appeal to our disappearing middle class?"

Sanders was even more of a misfit in the Senate than he was in the House. In a legislative body of 435, one can blend in or get lost. In the 100-member debating society of the Senate, you might expect one to have a greater presence and impact. But Senator Sanders didn't accomplish much at first. As he had in the House, he introduced much legislation and delivered hours of speeches, but few of his efforts turned into law, and his oratory often had little effect. According to Congress.gov, Sanders introduced 2,174 pieces of legislation from the time he became a senator in 2007 through 2015.

He sponsored or cosponsored 1,307 bills and introduced 604 amendments. Only thirty-five of these became law.

Senator Sanders did manage to have an impact on President Obama's Affordable Care Act. From 2008 to 2010, leading up to passage of the Affordable Care Act, Obama and the Democrats conducted a careful, sometimes desperate balancing act to ensure that they had a supermajority of sixty votes in order to shorten debate on the health care bill and pass it. Including Sanders and Connecticut's Joe Lieberman, the other Independent in the Senate, the Democrats had fifty-nine votes at the end of the 2008 elections. Then, on April 28, 2009, Republican Arlen Specter changed parties, giving the Democrats their much-needed sixtieth vote. The rest of 2009 would be a back-and-forth across the supermajority line. On August 25 Democrat Ted Kennedy of Massachusetts died, and on September 25 Democrat Paul Kirk was appointed interim senator for Massachusetts until a special election could be held in 2010. This meant that on December 24 the Senate was able to avoid a Republican filibuster and pass the Affordable Care Act, 60 to 39.

Sanders, the longtime advocate of single-payer, government-financed health insurance, had not supported the Affordable Care Act because it would contract out health insurance to private companies. But Democrats needed Sanders to maintain their supermajority, which gave him a lot of negotiating power. He used his leverage to get $11 billion devoted to expanding community health centers in all states. His amendment would eventually lead to grants from the Health and Human Services Department to be split among sixty-seven community health centers to open new locations and provide health care to an additional 286,000 people. The amendment also enabled health centers to provide primary care to patients regardless of their ability to pay. Sanders also used his leverage to stop efforts by Republicans and some Democrats to cut Social Security funding.

Senator Sanders was beginning to gain his footing.

★ ★ ★

The senator was a man of routine. He lived a Spartan life— the proverbial all work and no play. According to his staff, he rarely slacked off. When he wasn't working on a speech, attending meetings, or preparing for hearings, he was reading reports that gave him additional ammunition for his endless harangue: the rich were getting richer, the middle class was disappearing, and more Americans were falling below the poverty line.

Sanders himself was solidly in the middle class, which put him in the minority in the Senate, a lair of millionaires. Aside from a Burlington condominium valued at $100,000 to $250,000, the website *Money Nation* claims Sanders had just $31,000 to $115,000 tucked in a credit union and a retirement account in 2015. His net worth of $528,014 ranked him eighty-sixth among his colleagues in terms of wealth.

On most mornings Sanders would rise at around 8:00, walk a block to work around 9:00, and eat a breakfast of oatmeal and coffee at the Dirksen Senate Office Building across Constitution Avenue from the Supreme Court and the US Capitol. After breakfast he would meet with his staff. Then he would launch into his day. On most Fridays he could be found on the *Brunch with Bernie* radio show hosted by his friend Thom Hartmann, an internationally syndicated talk show host. "Bernie is a regular guest," the senator's website notes.

But on Friday, December 10, 2010, Sanders altered his routine. At 10:25 he walked onto the Senate floor and started delivering a speech. The chamber was virtually empty. There were no bills to debate or votes to take. Sanders had the floor to himself. By Senate rules, once a member has the floor and starts talking, he or she can keep talking—and talking and talking—provided the member doesn't yield the floor, unless he or she yields to a senator who then yields the floor back. The tactic, called a filibuster, is covered by the arcane Senate Rule XIX; senators use it to delay passage of legislation they find objectionable.

A few days before Sanders took the Senate floor, President Obama had broken through a budget impasse by making compromises with Republicans. Sanders found many parts of the bill extremely objectionable, and that Friday morning he wanted to explain why. "In my view," he began, "the agreement they reached is a bad deal for the American people. I think we can do better."

He then eviscerated the Tax Relief, Unemployment Insurance Reauthorization, and Job Creation Act of 2010, claiming it would cost $858 billion over ten years. He criticized a section of the bill that would provide tax breaks for the wealthiest Americans, another that would all but repeal the estate tax, and another that would extend President George W. Bush's tax rates for all incomes for another two years. But he didn't stop there. He kept talking for an hour, then for another, then through lunch—about which time senators and reporters began to realize that he might talk all day. C-SPAN beamed the speech live. Twitter lit up with Sanders's latest lines.

"By lunchtime his old-fashioned filibuster was a social-media sensation," Brian Stelter wrote in the *New York Times*, "with untold thousands of people commenting in real-time on Web sites like Twitter."

Sanders kept talking. His speech became a lecture, a recitation of statistics he'd been rolling out since Reagan was president, a diatribe on "the crooks on Wall Street," and finally a general jeremiad against greed.

"You can call what I am doing today whatever you want—you can call it a filibuster, you can call it a very long speech," he said at one point. "I'm not here to set any great records or to make a spectacle. I am simply here today to take as long as I can to explain to the American people the fact that we have got to do a lot better than this agreement provides."

He talked through the afternoon and into the evening.

"We should be embarrassed that we are not investing in our infrastructure, that we are not breaking up these large financial institutions, that we're not putting a cap on interest rates," he railed. "That we are the only country in the world that does not have health care for all of their people in major countries. We should be embarrassed."

Sanders's oratory continued to churn on social media. By Friday evening it topped Twitter's "trending topics" list. The *Huffington Post* reported that the video stream "became so popular that it temporarily shut down the Senate video server."

At around 6:45 p.m. Sanders called for "a better proposal which better reflects the needs of the middle class and working families of our country and, to me, most importantly, the children of our country."

At 6:59—after eight hours and thirty-five minutes—he looked up at the senator holding the gavel and said, "And with that, Madam President, I yield the floor."

When reporters asked why he stopped, he replied simply, "I'm tired."

Sanders's theatrics and eight-and-a-half-hour tutorial on the ills of the American economy failed to derail or alter the bipartisan budget deal Republicans and Democrats had reached the day before. True, President Obama had summoned Bill Clinton to the White House that Friday afternoon to draw some attention away from Sanders. But the Senate approved the deal on Monday.

Regardless of what transpired in Washington, Sanders stuck to his mantra "I work in Washington—I live in Vermont." After the daylong, solo speech, he headed home. Like every weekend he flew back to Burlington, toured the state, held meetings, and assembled constituents in town halls to discuss issues. In 2012 Vermonters reelected him with 71 percent of the vote.

Senator John McCain is a navy man from stem to stern. Both his father and his grandfather were admirals. He graduated from the Naval Academy and became an aviator. In a bombing mission over North Vietnam on October 26, 1967, McCain's plane was shot down. The force of the ejection knocked him unconscious and broke both of his arms and both of his legs. North Vietnamese captured him and imprisoned him in the notorious Hanoi Hilton prison, where he spent five and a half years as a prisoner of war and healed, to the extent possible in captivity.

On the basis of his military service and unwavering support for the Pentagon, McCain rose to power as a politician in Arizona. He's been a US senator since 1987 and ran for the White House in 2008. Sanders, meanwhile, had managed to avoid the Vietnam draft. He had built his political brand by running against the military and criticizing the defense budget during his sixteen years in the House and his decade as a senator.

Despite their clear differences, in the summer of 2014 an unexpected mix of politics and malfeasance threw the two together.

In April news broke in Phoenix that up to forty veterans had died while waiting for appointments with doctors at the local VA Hospital. That triggered investigations, which found that veterans across the country were forced to wait months before they got care at VA hospitals. In Phoenix, the VA inspector general reported, it was taking an average of 115 days for veterans to get basic care. Even more troubling, bureaucrats were falsifying records to make it appear that veterans were getting better, faster care.

The duty to investigate this scandalous situation and pass legislation to help needy veterans fell on Sanders, then chairman of the Senate Veterans Affairs Committee. Sanders proposed a bill that would open more health centers, adding billions to the VA budget. He prepared to negotiate with the ranking Republican on the committee, Senator Richard Burr of North Carolina. However, Burr, the son of a minister and himself a former sales manager for a lawn equipment company, declined to deal with Sanders.

The Republican leadership asked McCain to step in and work with Sanders, even though McCain was not on the Veterans Affairs Committee. The two had chatted over the years but had not worked together or developed a relationship. Now, closeted in a room in the Dirksen Senate Office Building, they hashed out details of a bill that would provide better treatment for America's veterans in the decades to come.

"Bernie was blunt," McCain says, "but I like that. He fought for what he believed in." How did the former navy airman and the once-rabid Vietnam War protester get along? "Famously. We fought over everything. But I found Senator Sanders to be an honorable man."

Writing for the Brookings Institution, journalist Jill Lawrence described their negotiations as "to a large extent a proxy for the two parties' epic, long-running battle over the size and role of the federal government and, in particular, its involvement in health care."

Sanders had spent his entire political life preparing to enter that fray.

★ ★ ★

Sanders had learned a harsh lesson in January 1991, when he returned to Vermont after voting against the resolution supporting US troops in the Persian Gulf War. He arrived at the VFW Hall in downtown Burlington, mounted the stage, took the podium, and stared out as every veteran in the packed house turned his back on him.

The message was clear: Support the troops or you'll pay for it.

Sanders was deeply hurt, in part because he revered veterans. Like workers and farmers, they fit into his vision of middle-class Americans who made great sacrifices only to be shafted by the system in return. He tried to explain his vote as a protest against President Bush's rush to war. He also promised to protect their interests, and from then on he ordered his staff to establish and maintain strong ties to Vermont veterans and their organizations. When he became chairman of the Senate Veterans Affairs Committee in 2013—his first full committee chairmanship—he noted that the first bill he had introduced in Congress, back in 1991, called for reimbursing members of the National Guard and Reserve for wages and income they lost while deployed in Operation Desert Storm.

As chair of the Committee, he was well aware that veterans were not getting the best or fastest care from Veterans Administration hospitals. The VA health care system is the country's largest, with an estimated 1,600 medical centers, clinics, and other facilities. Its annual budget is around $55 billion, and it can register as many as 288,000 appointments daily. In her article for Brookings, Jill Lawrence reported Sanders's claim that some 2 million veterans who served in Iraq and Afghanistan enrolled in the VA in four years; half a million of them had returned with posttraumatic stress disorder or traumatic brain injury.

In May 2014, in response to the burgeoning VA hospital scandal, Sanders introduced his omnibus Veterans Affairs Bill, which he asserted would increase accountability by making it easier to fire high-ranking VA appointees. At a cost of $22 billion over ten years, the bill would also, he said, improve health care, education, and job training for veterans, and it would restore a 1 percent cost-of-living adjustment that had been withdrawn from military pensions. Veterans groups, including the VFW and American Legion, supported the bill. Republicans did not. Florida's senator Marco Rubio told Sanders on the Senate floor the bill was much too costly. "If you think it's too expensive to take care of our veterans," Sanders shot back, "then don't send them to war."

Sanders himself was about to go to war with Senator John McCain. McCain was well aware that the government system was failing many veterans, and he was "outraged" when news broke that veterans in his state were dying while waiting for appointments to see doctors at the VA hospital in Phoenix. "It was very emotional and painful for me, personally. It was also infuriating. We had been pointing out these problems for years."

Sanders expected McCain to introduce his own legislation, but without warning Sanders, McCain proposed enabling veterans to go outside the system to private doctors. Veterans would get a "choice card" they could use if they lived far away from a VA facility or had waited too long for an appointment, allowing them to use public funds to pay for private care.

Sanders blew up, privately and publicly. In his view, McCain was introducing the first step toward the eventual privatization of the VA. McCain, on the other hand, believed

Sanders wished to prop up the VA with unlimited amounts of federal funds: "Bernie wanted to build more clinics, spend more money, and expand services. We had no quarrel about taking care of veterans. We just had differing views on how to do that."

Word was that Sanders and McCain battled in every way short of hand-to-hand combat. "We had a fight over every-thing," McCain admits. "Given Bernie's personality, it became very colorful. He was blunt and aggressive but in an admira-ble way."

The conflict played out on Sanders's turf in the Veterans Affairs Committee quarters. The two senators had compro-mised and traded away most of their differences until only the choice cards separated them. There were times when Mc-Cain stood up, stalked to the door, and reached for the handle. "Wait a minute, goddammit," Sanders would yell, insisting he come back.

Their final compromise bill included McCain's choice cards for ailing vets; Sanders got more clinics and doctors, ex-panded services, and increased military pensions.

"I thought he behaved honorably," McCain says of Sand-ers. "It's an overrated thing that every senator is as good as his word. Bernie is as good as his word."

★ ★ ★

To get the Veterans Affairs Bill through Congress, Sanders was going to have to meld the legislation he and McCain had hammered out in the Senate with the House bill backed by its Veterans Affairs Committee chairman, Florida Republican

Jeff Miller. In some ways Miller fit the definition of Sanders's polar opposite even better than McCain. "Congress embodies American diversity in all its crazy glory," Jill Lawrence wrote, "but Miller and Sanders had to set some kind of record for temperamental, cultural, and ideological differences."

Miller represented Florida's First District, along the state's east coast—one of the most conservative congressional districts in the nation. He was a member of the Republican Study Committee, the most conservative group in the House until Tea Party congressmen formed the Freedom Caucus. A large man who worked as a real estate broker and deputy sheriff before getting into politics, Miller trumpeted his conservative views. The legislation that came out of his committee included McCain's choice cards, as well as cost-cutting programs and reduced funding. He was familiar with Sanders, having served with him in the House. "This will be interesting," he thought.

When the two began meeting, Miller was not encouraged. "Bernie always wanted more," he says, as in more money and services. "That was his starting point: more. Was more really needed, I asked, or could the VA be more efficient?"

Sanders charged that Republicans wanted to privatize the VA, and he refused to budge. Miller says Sanders was so sure that Republicans were out to kill the VA that it took weeks of meetings to convince him that was not their aim. After that "it became an easier path."

The VA threw a boulder in that path when the administrator said his agency needed another $17 billion to serve the increased number of veterans from Iraq and Afghanistan. Sanders saw that as another reason to add funds to his bill. He and Miller drew farther apart. Each side threatened to quit. Aides said they stopped talking to each other, though Miller disputes that, declaring, "We never stopped talking," despite their disagreements.

But they never stopped posturing. In dueling press conferences each side charged the other with sacrificing the welfare of veterans for partisan politics. McCain reentered the battle zone and helped bring Miller and Sanders back to the table: "I made the argument that what we had worked out was a very important first step, but we couldn't make all the reforms we wanted in one bill." In other words: Declare victory, vote it through, and send the bill to the president.

In the end both houses passed the joint legislation by huge margins, and President Obama signed it into law on August 7, 2014. The Veterans' Access to Care through Choice, Accountability, and Transparency Act was the most important and far-reaching piece of legislation passed by a Congress whose dysfunction rendered it all but incapable of legislating.

"This has by far been the hardest thing that I have ever had to do since I have been in the United States Congress," Sanders said before the Senate vote. "But the stakes in terms of the needs of millions of veterans were so high that we just worked very, very hard on it."

After the House vote Miller said, "As different as we are politically, we are both realists, and I know Senator Sanders wanted to solve the problem as much as I did. And he gave, and we gave. And that is what a [compromise] is all about."

Said McCain, "It's been a pleasure to do combat with him."

★ ★ ★

On August 14, 2014, Sanders invited voters to gather at the town hall in Cabot, a village in Vermont's midsection known for its cheese and ultra-liberal leanings. Israel had recently invaded Gaza, reduced many of its apartment buildings to rubble, and killed more than 2,000 civilians. The small, spare town hall meeting room was packed. The crowd was primed for conflict.

Sanders had always walked a fine line on Israel and the Middle East. In his younger, more radical days in the 1980s, he would occasionally take the position that Palestinians deserved their own state and that achieving that end might require that the United States withhold arms from Israel. But in the House and Senate, with some exceptions, he had fallen more closely into Israel's fold.

"How can you not take a position against Israel?" asked a woman who read a long statement about the war and what she called "atrocities." As she spoke, Sanders's shoulders rose toward his ears.

"My turn?" he asked. As he began to explain his position on Israel and the Middle East—which calls for a two-state solution—the woman rose again.

"Are you going to go further and end $30 billion going to Israel over the next ten years?" she asked.

Sanders said, "You have a situation where Hamas is sending missiles into Israel, and you know where some of those missiles are coming from? They're coming from populated areas. Hamas has very sophisticated tunnels into Israel for military purposes."

"Gazans have a right to exist!" a man yelled from the back of the room.

"Excuse me, shut up!" Sanders yelled back. "You don't have the microphone."

More mean words flew at the senator. He held up both hands. "This is called a democracy!" he shouted. "I am answering a question, and I do not want to be disturbed!"

A state trooper watched from the side. "You're going to arrest people?" someone asked Sanders.

"You have a right to your view," Sanders said. "Hamas is very clear. Their view is that Israel shouldn't have the right to exist."

"Bullshit!" a man in the back said. "Fuck Israel."

Sanders tried to deflect the animus by introducing ISIS as the new threat in the region, but the crowd brought the session back to Israel.

"I have been working on it for the last fifty years," Sanders said. "I'm sorry. I don't have the magic answer. This is a very depressing and difficult issue. This has gone on for sixty bloody years, year after year. . . . If you're asking me if I have the magical solution, I don't, and you know what? I doubt very much that you do."

★ ★ ★

After nearly a decade in the Senate, Sanders had few friends but more than a few admirers. His fellow senators had grudging respect for his honesty and consistency. Was he the most effective senator? Not by a long shot. The most productive in terms of getting legislation passed? Hardly. But he advocated for the working class and criticized the wealthy at every turn.

Sanders had what political strategists call a "safe seat."

Vermonters adored him and would elect him until he called it quits or fell face-forward while sticking it to the man. He would be up again in 2018, when he would be seventy-seven. With good health, he could run again and again.

But even back in 2013 people asked Sanders if he was interested in running for president. He seemed to enjoy the prospect—and toying with the questioner.

In an October 2013 *Playboy* interview, writer Jonathan Tasini asked, "Are you absolutely ruling out running for president, 100 percent?"

Sanders smiled. "Absolutely? 100 percent? Cross my heart? Is there a stack of Bibles somewhere?" he asked. "Look, maybe it's only 99 percent. I care a lot about working families. I care a lot about the collapse of the American middle class. I care a lot about the enormous wealth and income disparity in our country. I care a lot that poverty in America is near an all-time high but hardly anyone talks about it. I realize running for president would be a way to shine a spotlight on these issues that are too often in the shadows today."

He paused.

"But I am at least 99 percent sure I won't."

★ NINE ★

THE MISSIONARY

"Better to show up than to give up."
—BERNIE SANDERS, 2014

In April 2013 Burlington attorney John Franco was just back from a trip to Cuba with a group of students when he fielded an urgent call from his friend. "Can you come over?" Sanders asked. "I want to talk about a few things."

Franco had been in the Sanders "family" since 1974, when he was a college student agog at the charismatic New Yorker who was leading the Liberty Union Party. He helped run Sanders's first mayoral campaign and worked in his city hall as assistant city attorney. He worked to elect Sanders to Congress and served briefly on the staff of his DC office. Sanders trusted Franco, now white-haired but still boyish when it came to his love for Vermont and Bernie. They were not in frequent contact, but Sanders knew Franco continued to support him.

When Sanders phoned, Franco was settling in on a Sunday night. He asked what Sanders was calling about. The talk turned instead to Cuba and other topics. Then Sanders got closer to the point: "I have to make a political decision. I'm getting a few people together."

Franco drove to Sanders's modest home in Burlington's New North End, a development on a point of land jutting into Lake Champlain; the joke was that Sanders was the first socialist to have a swimming pool in his backyard. When Franco arrived he found a gathering of the inner circle: philosophy professor Richard Sugarman; Phil Fiermonte, who had run Sanders's Vermont outreach operation for years; Hank "Huck" Gutman, a University of Vermont English professor who had cowritten with Sanders *Outsider in the House*; and Jane O'Meara Sanders, the senator's wife and political confidante. It didn't escape Franco that the group resembled the 1980 gathering in the Franklin Square public housing project at which Sanders first decided to run for mayor.

Like all gatherings at Sanders's place, there was no wine, beer, or booze—just brownies and decaf coffee. At first the conversation meandered from spring plantings to summer plans, as might be expected at a meeting of longtime friends. They might have been devotees in the cult of Bernie—"Sanderistas" in local parlance—but each was bright, experienced, and politically savvy. They knew Sanders and cared about him. They were invested in him and his mission. And they all wondered why he had summoned them.

"I am considering a run for the White House in 2016," Sanders said about a half hour into the session. "I want to get a sense of what you think."

There was quiet at first, then the group began to dissect the idea. They agreed that Sanders's constant and long-standing outrage over income inequality would reach a receptive audience nationwide. The Occupy Wall Street protests that began in 2011 had run their course, but they had pushed "income inequality" into the national conversation. All of a sudden politicians and TV anchors were talking about the "1 percent" of Americans in whom all the wealth was concentrated. Hadn't Sanders coined the 1 percent in his 1996 reelection campaign against Susan Sweetser?

Jane wondered about giving up even more privacy. She knew that a presidential campaign would bring unfettered intrusions by the press and opposition.

Sanders wondered about his age. "You know, I'm seventy-two," he pointed out. "Am I too old?"

They scoffed. Everyone knew that he was indefatigable. Franco weighed in with a tale about the coach of his college cross-country ski team. "'If you're not throwing up after crossing the finish line, you're not giving it everything,' he would say and ask, 'What are you saving it for?'"

Franco looked at Sanders. "So what are you saving it for?"

Sanders wouldn't make a decision until a year or more down the road, but he wanted to begin the process by sharing his thoughts with and seeking the counsel of trusted friends. The conversation was more introspective than prospective, but they all expressed their support.

After the meeting Sanders took Sugarman aside. "What should I do?"

"Are you asking me as a citizen or a friend?" Sugarman asked.

"As a friend," Sanders replied. "I don't have that many friends."
"I don't know what to tell you," Sugarman said. "But if you do run, you'd better be running to win."

★ ★ ★

What motivated Sanders to consider running for president in the spring of 2013, two years before a campaign would begin? He had just been elected to a second six-year term as senator, an exalted position by any measure. He was about to take charge of the Veterans Affairs Committee, which would give him the power to help millions of men and women who mattered to him. He had a loving wife, four children, and eight grandchildren. Why would he put himself and his family through the rigors of a yearlong presidential campaign? Why risk getting no traction and looking like a fool?

Sanders, who almost never comments publicly about personal matters, did not make himself available for this book. So we are left to ponder.

In the beginning, when he stumbled and stammered through his first political venture in 1971, he told people he wasn't a politician. Sylvia Manning, who had met Sanders at the initial Liberty Union meeting and lived near him in Burlington, accompanied him to his first TV panel discussion in his first race for one of Vermont's US Senate seats. She had this to say: "He ran so he could get air time, not to win but to educate people. He thought of himself as the educational candidate."

Sanders could not have had any illusions about winning any of the four races he ran for statewide office in the 1970s. But he could express his views about the economy and foreign affairs, and he discovered that he could command a crowd. He talked; people listened. Through his upbringing in Brooklyn, his reading at the University of Chicago, and his time on the Israeli kibbutz, he had developed a set of core values that revolved around his respect for the ordinary people who did the work, tilled the fields, fought the wars. He dismissed adherents of the New Left as elitists; instead he connected with the 1930s socialists and their edification of the working class.

Even at the early stages of Sanders's political development he grounded his campaigns in economic justice and class conflict. He became a true believer in his own mission to save the working class, which grew into his mission to save the middle class. Either way, Sanders was on a mission.

He had been reluctant to run for mayor of Burlington in 1980, in part because he wasn't sure how it would advance his mission. It turned out to be a valuable step, in that he learned the practical aspects of leadership. And he was able to actually improve the lives of Burlington's poor and working class. "He tried to apply his broader economic outlook to the local level," says David Clavelle, who worked on Sanders's campaign and then in his city administration. Linda Niedweske, who managed Sanders's first campaign and also worked in his administration, recalls that he didn't have time to dally or coddle people. "He's always been on a mission," says Niedweske, now a lawyer in New Jersey. "He has no time for much else."

In some ways Sanders's eight years and four terms as mayor were a hiatus, a pause between realizing his mission and executing it. He was always looking for a bigger platform: first governor, then congressman, then senator.

When Vermonters realized Sanders was not the "fluke"

that the establishment hoped he was, they wondered which political party he would join. He had run for Liberty Union. He called himself a socialist and had even served as a Socialist Workers Party elector in 1980. He'd run as an Independent for mayor. There wasn't much chance he would become a Democrat, but there was some expectation that he would join the Progressive Party that had started to elect Burlington aldermen. But Sanders declined.

"Bernie became his own party, his own brand," says David Clavelle. "No question about it."

But that begs a broader question.

Sanders rode his *sui generis* political brand to Congress so he could continue his mission. Read any of the speeches he's given in the House and Senate. In almost every utterance he is pressing for workers' rights, a higher minimum wage, economic justice, and saving the middle class.

Then, in 2013, he added a new goal to his mission. He started exhorting people to join together and mount a grassroots movement for change. In this enhanced version of his basic stump speech, Sanders declared that no one person— no leader, no president—could force the change necessary to reverse the country's headlong trajectory toward greater and more destructive income inequality. It would take a "political revolution," which would not take place until "millions of people showed up in Washington, DC, and said, 'Enough is enough!'"

But to decide whether to run for the White House he would have to take his mission on the road. "We were concerned about the direction of the economy and the widening gap between the very rich and everyone else," Jane says. "But were people as concerned as we were?" Would Americans, beyond the close friends in his living room, join his mission?

Bernie and Jane ventured beyond Vermont to find out.

Traveling by themselves—no staff, no advance team—they quietly set up meetings around the country throughout 2014. She describes their trip to Arizona as particularly valuable: "We stopped in various little towns, visited community health centers. We stopped in schools. We called mayors to say he would be in town. Not just Democrats or Independents or Progressives, but people all over the place. We stopped by to visit with veterans groups. No one ever turned us down."

Those trips helped Sanders determine whether to make a run. "We found quite a synergy between his concerns, Vermonters' concerns, and the concerns of people in the rest of the country," says Jane. Many of the people they encountered agreed that the middle class was suffering and the gap between the wealthy and the rest of the country was becoming intolerable.

Sanders was primed. "Better to show up than to give up," he would say.

But his wife was still reticent, and he respected her point of view. He agreed to forgo a presidential run if she advised against it.

In the fall of 2014 Sanders took a long walk through downtown Burlington with Jim Rader, his political touchstone since his college days in Chicago. Rader had known Sanders for fifty years, worked for him in Burlington and in his congressional office. Sanders told Rader he wanted to provide an alternative to Hillary Clinton, but his mind was not made up. Rader just listened.

On the morning of April 18, 2015, Jane and Bernie were having breakfast at a Denny's in South Burlington. The conversation turned once again to whether Sanders should run or not. Jane presented her concerns: she was worried about the energy it would take, the rigors of campaigning, the hassle of raising money, and the effect on their personal lives. As Sanders began making his case for running, a disabled veteran approached.

"I don't mean to interrupt," he said, according to Jane, "but I hear you are considering running for president. I hope you do."

He said he had tried to get his VA benefits for thirty years with no success. Then he called Sanders's office for assistance, and his staff had helped him navigate the bureaucracy and unlock the funds. "You've changed my life," he said, "and if you run for president, I think that would be the best thing for the country. I'll do anything for you." He thanked the couple and excused himself.

"I give up," Jane said. "You're right—we have to do this."

On April 29 Sanders alerted his friends and allies by email that he intended to run: "After a year of travel, discussion, and dialogue, I have decided to be a candidate for the Democratic nomination for president." He said he was spurred on by economic inequality, climate change, and the *Citizens United* Supreme Court decision. He confirmed his intentions to the Associated Press: "People should not underestimate me. I've run outside of the two-party system, defeating Democrats and Republicans, taking on big-money candidates, and, you know,

I think the message that has resonated in Vermont is a message that can resonate all over this country."

Sugarman and Franco were pumped. "We gave up running symbolic campaigns long ago," Sugarman says. "He's not in this to give a speech at the convention. He's in it to win."

Says Franco, "Bernard thrives on being discounted and ignored."

TEN

THE POPULIST

"He's simply not talking about socialism, then."
—Tim Worstall

John F. Kennedy Jr. revered Abraham Lincoln, the president who went to war to end slavery. Bill Clinton's mentor was Arkansas senator J. William Fulbright, whose eponymous scholarship program sponsors exchange of academics between the US and foreign countries. Bernard Sanders idolizes Eugene V. Debs, perhaps the most charismatic and successful socialist politician in US history.

A plaque honoring Debs is one of the first things visitors to Sanders's office in the Russell Senate Office Building are likely to see. Sanders has been a Debs devotee since he was a college kid reading Trotsky in the basement of the University of Chicago library. Before he was Burlington's mayor, he produced, narrated, and marketed a twenty-eight-minute documentary

titled *Eugene V. Debs: Trade Unionist, Socialist, Revolutionary,*
1855–1926. "Debs is my model," he often told friends.

Eugene Debs was a homegrown socialist from Kansas.
He helped found the Socialist Party of America in 1901 and
led it for the next two decades. Campaigning for president in
1908, he whistle-stopped the country in a "Red Special" railcar
filled with posters, reporters, and party members. He stopped
in small towns to give raucous speeches that drew thousands.
At its height the party had 150,000 members. Debs ran for
president five times, peaking in 1912, when he and his socialist
ticket pulled in almost 6 percent of the vote.

"Much like Bernie Sanders, Debs could inspire a crowd,"
Greg Guma wrote in the progressive publication *Toward Free-*
dom. Debs could be amusing, "but his target was always the
same—big capitalists and their bankers, judges, politicians, ed-
itors, and even conservative union leaders. He called on workers to join a moral struggle against 'wage slavery.'"

Sanders is not shy about his admiration of Debs, but he's
not as forthcoming about the importance of socialism in his life
and political development. Running for president, he tries to
avoid being tagged a socialist. He prefers "democratic socialist."

What has socialism meant to Sanders? How does he fit
into the history of socialism in America? How do socialists
feel about him? More important, will America elect a socialist
president?

★ ★ ★

The senator promised to clear up his brand of socialism at
a speech at Georgetown University on November 19, 2015.

Inside Gaston Hall, jammed with adoring students, Sanders cloaked himself in the mantles of Franklin Delano Roosevelt and Martin Luther King Jr. He pointed out that when FDR established Social Security, the minimum wage, and the forty-hour workweek and outlawed child labor, opponents labeled each measure "socialistic."

President Johnson's Medicare and Medicaid? "Socialistic," Sanders declared. "Martin Luther King used to say, 'This country has socialism for the rich and rugged individualism for the poor.'"

A half hour into his ninety-minute address, Sanders began to outline his definition of socialism. "I don't believe government should take over the grocery store down the street or own the means of production," he explained, eschewing basic Marxist dogma. "But I do believe that the middle class and the working families who produce the wealth of America deserve a decent standard of living and that their incomes should go up, not down."

In other words, Bernard Sanders is in no way a classic Socialist, by any measure. "Socialism is a social and economic system characterized by social ownership and democratic control of the means of production," according to Wikipedia.

"He's simply not talking about socialism then," writes *Forbes* contributor Tim Worstall. "Because socialism is absolutely predicated upon the idea that, this is the one single point that makes it unique, government and or the workers should own the means of production. If you're not arguing for that then you're not arguing for socialism."

So what is Sanders arguing for? The short answer is populism, which is much easier to digest and has a long and respected history in American politics. Begun with farmers in the Midwest, populists advocated for the interests of ordinary people against those of the privileged elite. Sound like Bernie Sanders?

Starting with William Jennings Bryan, "the great commoner," who won the Democratic nomination for president in 1896, populists and their heirs—today's progressives—have had a voice in US politics, at times strong, at others muted. Bryan lost to William McKinley, but his brand of advocating for the farmers and workers against the wealthy won over many Americans. You can find populist rage fueling leaders such as three-time New York Mayor Fiorella La Guardia, Louisiana Senator Huey Long, Bobby Kennedy, former Texas governor Anne Richards, and even US Senator Barbara Mikulski, whose political base rests with Baltimore's steel workers.

If Sanders's watered-down version of socialism sounds more like populism or far-left liberalism, that was not always the case. As a college student and freshly minted Vermont politician, he had been more of a hardcore socialist.

"Socialism is the heart and soul of Sanders's life," Steven Soifer wrote in his 1981 book, *Socialist Mayor*. When interviewed by Soifer, Sanders defined socialism as "a vision of society where poverty is absolutely unnecessary, where international relations are not based on greed . . . but on cooperation [and] . . . where human beings own the means of production and work together rather than having to work as semi-slaves to other people who can hire and fire."

Back then Sanders could see himself becoming among the most influential American socialists, like his idol, Debs.

★ ★ ★

The first Socialists in America were, essentially, hippies. They established utopian communities of the early nineteenth century such as the Shakers, New Harmony in Indiana, and Brook Farm outside of Boston. Based on European models, they were attempts to create farming communities built on the principles of shared work and communal decisions. They were precursors to the Israeli kibbutz and American communes of the 1960s and 1970s. And they failed.

Europeans, primarily Germans, brought socialist doctrine to the United States after the revolutions of 1848 against continental monarchies. But it wasn't until later in the century that political parties, such as the Socialist Labor Party, took shape in America. US socialist parties borrowed from European ideology, based on the teachings of Karl Marx and others, which held that workers should own the large corporations and control the government for the good of the general public. The American model was based on democratic socialism, in that reform would take place through the ballot box rather than violent revolutions that overthrew monarchies in Russia and China.

After World War II Joseph Stalin turned Russia and its satellites into the Union of Soviet Socialist Republics (USSR). For the next forty-five years the United States and its allies contended with the Soviet Union and China in a cold war of arms and ideology. Communism and socialism were seen as competing with capitalism for world domination. Led by rabid anticommunists like Wisconsin congressman Joe McCarthy, Congress forced purges of suspected communists in Washington and Hollywood. More than a few members of the creative class in the film industry had left-wing leanings, and any association with communism led to their being "black-listed" and shunned.

Communism and, by association, socialism became anathema in the United States. But socialism's fundamental tenet—that the fruits of labor should be shared more evenly—continued to attract writers, educators, and political leaders. If capitalism represents economic survival of the fittest, socialism calls on government to see that wealth is distributed across economic divides. In many ways socialism shares Christianity's basic belief in the importance of caring for those in need.

When Sanders was growing up in Brooklyn, socialist trade unions and communist organizations were part of the neighborhood's fabric. Many Jewish communists migrated from Europe and settled in and around New York. Their children, members of Sanders's generation, were known as "red-diaper babies."

Sanders was not part of that sect. Except for tagging along with his brother, Larry, to a few political meetings, he seems to have grown up without much political influence. He has said that his parents were not involved in politics and that dinner discussions rarely touched on political subjects. Nonetheless, Brooklyn was FDR country. President Roosevelt wanted to put the Great Depression in the country's rearview mirror and get Americans back to work, and the ethnic communities in and around Flatbush were eager to take advantage of every opportunity to get ahead. What Sanders absorbed from his Brooklyn upbringing was more economic than political. He saw his father and other men working hard yet struggling to make ends meet.

The Russian Revolution also captivated young Sanders.

He fell for the Bolsheviks. It is not surprising that a curious
college student in the 1960s would gravitate toward leftist
causes. Marxist professors taught socialism and encouraged
radicalism. Students wanted power to engage in "free speech"
and stage protests to express their rage against the Vietnam
War, discrimination, and injustice. Sanders studied original
socialist texts and put their teachings into practice by protesting against racism and for affordable housing and better public
education. "That was probably the major period of intellectual
ferment in my life," he told the *Vermont Vanguard* in 1981.
Socialism infused that ferment.

   In Vermont Sanders's socialist predilections blossomed. He
was campaigning for office and running his own show, literally. He used his position to rail against imperialism and advocate public ownership of utilities. He built ties to the Socialist
Workers Party and became an elector for its presidential slate
in 1980. But when he ran for mayor of Burlington that same
year, he scrubbed "socialist" from his talking points and stump
speeches. If political affiliation came up, he described himself as
an Independent, albeit a very progressive one. His alliance with
the patrolman's association inoculated him from attacks from
the right. But at his swearing-in he gave a speech on economic
equality—that is, socialism—that would be familiar to anyone
who has heard him in the subsequent thirty-five years:

   In America today, the rich are getting richer, the poor are
   getting poorer, and the millions of families in the middle are gradually sliding out of the middle class and into
   poverty.
      In the final analysis the people of America are going

to have to say that the wealth, labor, and natural resources must be used to benefit all the people, not just a
few super-rich.

But Sanders reassured Burlington's corporate leaders that
he wanted to work with them and had no "great sadistic desire" to destroy the business community. Keep in mind that
he sided with General Electric when peace protestors tried to
shut down the Burlington plant.

Even so, as mayor Sanders worked to have the municipal
government help redistribute wealth in Burlington. He increased taxes; he used city funds to improve public housing;
and he extended the city's resources to rundown communities.
Call it democratic socialism in practice.

"I am a socialist; of course I am a socialist," he said in a
1983 reelection debate covered by the AP. "To hold a vision
that society can be fundamentally different, to believe that all
people can be equal, that is not a new idea."

No, it's an old idea that goes back to the Declaration of
Independence. And it's not socialism.

When Sanders ran for Congress in 1988 and 1990 he once
again expunged the "S" word from his résumé and record. He
ran as Bernie, the progressive Independent whom Vermonters
had gotten to know and appreciate. But reporters did ask him
to explain his political leanings after an opponent's ad linked
him to Fidel Castro. "I am a socialist and everyone knows
that," he told reporters in 1990. "They also understand that
my democratic socialism has nothing to do with authoritarian
communism."

Every time Sanders got elected, some reporter somewhere "discovered" that a socialist had just been elected to Congress, and a story about the "socialist in the Senate" would appear.

When pressed in his Senate days, he frequently explained that his brand of socialism was similar to the kind one might find in Finland and Sweden. Appearing on *The Colbert Report* in 2008, Sanders said, "The reality is there are many countries in Scandinavia and Europe who have done things like provide health care to every man, woman, and child as a right to citizenship."

> STEPHEN COLBERT: Need I remind you this is not Scandinavia or Europe?
> SANDERS: Need I remind you we have forty-seven million Americans without any health insurance, and we spend twice as much as any country?
> COLBERT: That's class warfare. You're talking about redistribution of wealth.
> SANDERS: I am.

★ ★ ★

What worked for Stephen Colbert was not working for some of America's hardcore socialists.

"Bernie Sanders is no Eugene Debs," blared the May 26, 2015, headline on SocialistWorker.org, an outlet of the International Socialist Organization. Of Sanders's presidential run, activist Howie Hawkins wrote, "Bernie Sanders' entry into the Democratic presidential primaries should be seen as his final decisive step away from the democratic socialism he professes to support. He will raise some progressive demands in the primaries and then endorse the corporate Democrat, Hillary Clinton. Nothing changes."

"Sanders is violating the first principle of socialist politics: class independence," Hawkins added. "The socialist movement learned that principle long ago when business classes sold out the workers in the democratic revolutions of 1848 that swept across Europe and parts of Latin America."

In an earlier SocialistWorker.org article, the writer argued, "Setting aside his self-identification as a 'socialist,' even his claim to be 'independent' is dubious once you know about Sanders' accommodations with business and the wealthy and his ongoing collaboration with the Democratic Party."

Which begs the question, why did Sanders run as a Democrat rather than as an Independent? First, Sanders is a pragmatist. Like William Jennings Bryan in 1896, he knows that the best chance of actually getting elected president is through one of the two main parties. An Independent can win in Vermont but stands no chance on the national stage. Second, Sanders has no intention of playing the spoiler, as Ralph Nader did in 2000, when he drew votes from Al Gore and helped elect George W. Bush.

Meanwhile, not all socialists agreed with the harsh judgment that Sanders is a fraud. "I think having that word in the discourse, it can help sort of stimulate a positive response, as the stigma wears off," Mimi Soltysik of the Socialist Party USA told Bloomberg Politics. "So let's say, hypothetically, that

Bernie Sanders doesn't defeat Hillary Clinton in the primary. We'll still have a lot more people who know what [the word 'socialism'] means. That's a positive."

Still, the Socialist Party USA doesn't consider Sanders a real socialist. Why? Soltysik says democratic socialists believe in "community control of institutions" rather than private control, "local control of the means of production," and a socialized medical program. "And we're anti-capitalist. We don't see capitalism as a reformable institution."

Sanders buys the socialized medical program, but he rejects the rest.

★ ★ ★

In the balance Sanders is caught between capitalists skeptical of his claim that he's a democratic socialist and socialists who see him as a capitalist pawn.

"I don't find the semantic debates involved in this question very edifying," says Jack Ross, author of *The Socialist Party of America: A Complete History*. "That said, what is very clear to me is that Bernie's implicit critique fits in squarely with that of an older, lost liberalism, typified by the heyday of Americans for Democratic Action, which owes much indeed to the historic American Socialist tradition."

"Bottom line," Ross says, "I cannot emphasize enough or too strongly how much of what makes Bernie distinctive is a reflection of the politics that defined the left that forged him at Chicago in the peak years of the civil rights movement and the unvarnished small-d democratic and egalitarian spirit which he kept alive isolated in Vermont. And I believe that Bernie's time has come in this cycle precisely because the country is facing such severe problems of income inequality, broken public policy, and continued fallout from the foreign disasters of the Bush years at the very time the unholy marriage of the cultural revolutionary mob and the corporate liberal elite is setting the tone for so much of our politics."

Lane Kenworthy, a professor of sociology at the University of California at San Diego who recently wrote *Social Democratic America*, offers a convoluted description of Sanders: "He is, if you want to put it this way, a democratic socialist capitalist."

Which means that Sanders is not a socialist.

It's clear that Sanders has created his own distinct brand of socialist doctrine. It is democratic socialism in that he believes change will come through the ballot rather than by violent overthrow of the ruling class. He adheres to a tame socialism practiced in many European nations that provide free health care for all, superior public education, and generous pensions. But he does exhort the masses to rise up—at least figuratively—and bring about a political revolution.

Sanders's brand of socialism is not Trotskyism or 1930s-style socialism or a socialism accepted by the Socialist Workers Party. It accepts capitalism but demands that it bend to the benefit of the poor and middle class. It's more like the democratic socialism practiced in the Scandinavian nations, but not exactly.

Whatever Sanders means in his slippery identification with socialism, will the "masses" consider electing a candidate

who has called himself a socialist—even a democratic socialist? A Gallup poll released in June 2015 reported that 50 percent of American voters said they would not vote for a socialist
nominee for president.

Bernie Sanders puts little stock in polls.

★ ELEVEN ★

THE PROSELYTIZER

"Good news from Iowa—I'm only forty-eight points behind."
—BERNIE SANDERS, 2015

O n November 13, 2015, terrorists turned a lovely Paris evening into a nightmare. Brandishing automatic weapons, they opened fire on sidewalk cafés, set off bombs outside a soccer stadium, and gunned down a hundred rock music fans attending a concert at the Bataclan theater. The bloody attacks shocked the Western world. Was anyone anywhere safe from terrorists unafraid of dying in pursuit of barbaric goals set by ISIS leaders in Syria and Iraq?

The next night—with reports of the terrorist attacks dominating the news—the three candidates vying for the 2016 Democratic presidential nomination debated one another at Drake University in Des Moines, Iowa. Former secretary of state Hillary Rodham Clinton, favored in polls, stood between Senator Sanders and former Maryland governor Martin O'Malley. The three bowed their heads and observed a moment of silent prayer for the fallen and the survivors.

Then the moderator, CBS's John Dickerson, called on Sanders to offer his opening remarks.

"Well, John," Sanders began, his face bearing his trademark scowl, "let me concur with you and with all Americans who are shocked and disgusted by what we saw in Paris yesterday. Together, leading the world, this country will rid our planet of this barbarous organization called ISIS."

And that was it for terrorism, French blood flowing, and foreign affairs.

"I'm running for president because as I go around this nation, I talk to a lot of people," Sanders continued. "And what I hear is people's concern that the economy we have is a rigged economy. People are working longer hours for lower wages, and almost all of the new income and wealth goes to the top one percent."

This was, of course, familiar territory for Sanders. He needed no notes or teleprompter for a speech he had been giving in one form or another since 1981.

"And then on top of that we've got a corrupt campaign-finance system in which millionaires and billionaires are pouring huge sums of money into super PACs heavily influencing the political process. What my campaign is about is a political revolution—millions of people standing up and saying enough is enough. Our government belongs to all of us, and not just the handful of billionaires."

No surprises there. Sanders was focused, as always, on the

issues he reprised in his rhetoric at every opportunity. How did his competitors present themselves to the thousands in the audience at the university and millions tuning in by TV and Internet?

"Well," Clinton began, "our prayers are with the people of France tonight, but that is not enough." She called ISIS "a barbaric, ruthless, violent jihadist terrorist group." Then she used the news of the day as an opportunity to set herself apart from Sanders and present herself as a firm leader—even of the military: "This election is not only about electing a president. It's also about choosing our next commander in chief. And I will be laying out in detail what I think we need to do with our friends and allies in Europe and elsewhere to do a better job of coordinating efforts against the scourge of terrorism. Our country deserves no less, because all of the other issues we want to deal with depend upon us being secure and strong."

O'Malley called ISIS and its brand of terrorism "the new face of conflict and warfare in the twenty-first century." He concluded his opening remarks with this statement: "As a former mayor and a former governor, there was never a single day, John, when I went to bed or woke up without realizing that this could happen in our own country. We have a lot of work to do, to better prepare our nation and to better lead this world into this new century."

Up to this point in the presidential campaign Sanders had confounded the political prognosticators. The TV talking heads, the political science professors, the strategists and consultants—all had deemed him a short-timer in the race, even a curiosity. At best, they agreed, the senator from a small, rural state might draw the momentary fancy of voters who hungered for a left-wing alternative to Clinton. They said he was the beneficiary of Massachusetts senator Elizabeth Warren's decision to not run for the presidency. She, not Sanders, was the darling of the liberals. Looking back in time for models, they compared him to Senator Eugene McCarthy, who ran as an antiwar candidate in 1968 and whose largely amiable campaign had peaked in the summer and faded in the fall.

But the prognosticators were wrong.

The race for the 2016 Democratic nomination had begun with five candidates. In addition to Clinton, O'Malley, and Sanders, former senator Jim Webb of Virginia gave it a try. A former military man, secretary of the navy, and novelist, Webb could have been a contender, but his campaign never took off, and he dropped out after the first debate. Likewise former Rhode Island governor and US senator Lincoln Chafee didn't make it past the first debate. And though O'Malley remained in the running, he failed to attract much support.

As the months of primary voting approached, the Democratic race was down to two: Clinton and Sanders. Everyone pegged Sanders as the long shot. He was okay with that.

★ ★ ★

The primary races on the Republican side began with a crowd and careened from the comic to the bizarre. At the outset pundits believed it was Jeb Bush's race to lose. The former Florida governor stood to inherit the millions in campaign contributions and establishment GOP support that had helped elect his father and brother to the White House. But things didn't quite work out that way.

Competitors for the Republican nomination numbered seventeen at one point, including governors Bobby Jindal, John Kasich, and Chris Christie, former governor and talk show host Mike Huckabee, and senators Lindsey Graham, Marco Rubio, and Ted Cruz. But it was billionaire businessman and television showman Donald Trump and retired neurosurgeon Ben Carson who caught the initial fancy of Republican voters. Neither was a professional politician, and many voters saw that in a positive light. Republican activists threw spitballs at the GOP establishment by lining up behind candidates who could appeal to ultraconservative, anti-Washington voters.

Trump fit the bill—and led in the polls through the summer and fall. In reaction to the terrorist attacks that brought down a Russian civilian airliner and killed scores of people in Lebanon and Paris, Trump suggested that the United States keep a database of Muslims in the country; as for military strategy, he would "knock the hell out of ISIS." For his part, Carson compared the tide of Syrian refugees fleeing their war-torn nation to the threat posed by a "rabid dog" and suggested that the United States close its doors to them.

The conventional wisdom suggested that the GOP nomination was Trump's to win, with Rubio likely to present the best challenge.

The Democratic primary, on the other hand, was Clinton's to lose. She had the political apparatus and experience from her 2008 run. She had amassed the big dollars in campaign contributions. She brought a strong résumé as first lady, US senator, and secretary of state. She would be the first female president. With terrorism on the minds of voters, Clinton had foreign affairs experience and a reputation as a relative hawk.

But Sanders had what Clinton lacked: authenticity and the trust of supporters. To many Democrats Clinton came off as someone who changed her positions based on polls and politics rather than relying on her personal beliefs, her gut. Sanders, on the other hand, stated his positions and stuck to them. That was his strength. But when the public's attention turned to terrorism and foreign policy, it also proved a weakness and raised a crucial question: Could Bernie Sanders pivot? Or was he so strapped into his belief that economic justice trumped all else that it would become the cement shoes that dragged his campaign under?

★ ★ ★

The cement-shoes scenario seemed to be playing out in the November debate at Drake University, though Sanders tried to slip out of them.

In light of the 120 and counting killed in Paris, John Dickerson asked Sanders if he still believed that the greatest threat to national security was climate change, as he had said earlier. "Absolutely," Sanders responded. "In fact climate change is directly related to the growth of terrorism. And if we do not get our act together and listen to what the scientists say, you're going to see countries all over the world—this is what the CIA says—they're going to be struggling over limited amounts of water, limited amounts of land to grow their crops, and you're going to see all kinds of international conflict."

Dickerson questioned Sanders on his assertion that climate change caused terrorism, allowing him to shift from terrorism to his stronger suit, climate change. He wasn't entirely on shaky ground. Many scientists believe the warming of the earth will exacerbate poverty and provoke massive migration, both of which can contribute to terrorism. Sanders said a serious drought in Syria had forced farmers into the cities and contributed to the poor economy, which fed the ranks of terrorists. But he wasn't finished with Clinton; he aimed to inflict damage and weaken her lead. He criticized her for voting in favor of the invasion of Iraq when she was a senator: "I don't think any—I don't think any sensible person would disagree that the invasion of Iraq led to the massive level of instability we are seeing right now. I think that was one of the worst foreign policy blunders in the history of the United States."

For her part, Clinton acknowledged that "the invasion of Iraq was a mistake." Dickerson gave Sanders another swing by asking him, "Do you have anything to criticize in the way she performed as secretary of state?"

He did not, but he took the opportunity to pound her again anyway: "I think we have a disagreement, and the disagreement is that not only did I vote against the war in Iraq. If you look at history, John, you will find that regime change—whether it was in the early fifties in Iran, whether it was toppling Salvador Allende in Chile, whether it is overthrowing the government of Guatemala way back when—these invasions, these toppling of governments, regime changes have unintended consequences. I would say that on this issue, I'm a little bit more conservative than the secretary. And that I am not a great fan of regime change."

Sanders wasn't in favor of the United States leading the effort to combat terrorist groups like ISIS. "But here's something that I believe we have to do as we put together an international coalition," he said, "and that is we have to understand that the Muslim nations in the region—Saudi Arabia, Iran, Turkey, Jordan—all of these nations, they're going to have to get their hands dirty, their boots on the ground. They are going to have to take on ISIS."

Sanders managed to acquit himself adequately on foreign affairs, then he and O'Malley gave Clinton a tag-team thrashing for her close ties to Wall Street financiers, on whom she relied for both campaign cash and political advice. Sanders also noted that when her husband was in the White House, the treasury secretaries came from Wall Street. The debate moved on to Sanders's sweet spots: the "massive redistribution of wealth," ending corporate tax loopholes, instituting a tax on Wall Street speculation, raising the minimum wage to $15 an hour, making tuition free at public colleges. But he continued to aggressively press the issue of Clinton's Wall Street relationships: "Here's the story, I mean, you know, let's not be naïve about it. Why do—why, over her political career, has Wall Street been a major—*the* major—campaign contributor to Hillary Clinton? You know, maybe they're dumb and they don't know what they're going to get, but I don't think so."

That was one of Sanders's many applause lines during the debate. But in the end, though he nicked Clinton on her Wall Street ties, he lost to her on foreign policy, war, and terrorism—her strong suits. When the question was how the next president would protect Americans from terrorists hell-bent on destroying them and their way of life, Sanders kept steering the debate back to his territory: economic inequality and domestic affairs.

Three months before primary voting commenced, Sanders

needed to perform strongly enough to dent Clinton's commanding lead in the polls. He did not.

★ ★ ★

As Sanders had risen in the polls and attracted more people to his events, it became clear that he had a black problem. Some would say he had a people problem. Though protesting discrimination against black students at the University of Chicago had been one of his first causes, black faces were rare among the crowds that cheered on his presidential quest. Mainstream African American political groups and the majority of black voters favored Clinton, in part by association with her husband, Bill.

Sanders might have helped his cause by appealing to younger African American voters, but he blew a major opportunity to do so.

In the summer of 2015 larger and larger crowds filled arenas and auditoriums to hear the senator from Vermont rage against the economic system. In August he stepped onto the stage at the Netroots Nation convention in Phoenix. Thousands of young, digital natives filled the hall. As Sanders launched into his stump speech, chants rose from the audience: "Black lives matter" and "Say her name!"

During the previous six months news reports and social media had focused the nation's attention on African Americans who had died in police custody, often for little apparent reason and from officers' excessive use of force. They included Michael Brown in Ferguson, Missouri; Freddie Gray in Baltimore; and Sandra Bland in Hempstead, Texas. Activists under the "Black Lives Matter" banner staged protests across the country, including in Phoenix.

When the chants interrupted Sanders, he conferred with the moderator, journalist Jose Antonio Vargas. The two were alone on the stage. Then he faced the audience. "Let me talk about what I'm going to talk about for a second," he said. The chanting got louder. "Here's the serious issue: We live in a nation in which to a significant degree the media is controlled by large multinational—"

Chants of "Say her name, say her name!" drowned him out.

The activists wanted to hear Sanders speak about police killings and beatings of unarmed black men and women. Instead he tried to continue on script: "I want to give you some bad news and some good news."

Protestors took to the stage. Sanders walked off.

"Exasperating and classic Bernie," columnist Judith Levine wrote in *Seven Days*, Vermont's alternative newspaper. "Man of the people treating the people like tiresome children, telling them what the issue is, instead of listening to what their issue, our issue, America's issue is right now." Vargas called Sanders "tone deaf."

Was he not listening? Did he not want to hear?

Sanders has difficulty dealing with people who disagree with him. Among his faults, this could be the one that most seriously damages his presidential bid. Aides have called him strident and dissatisfied to the point of being abusive, especially during the 1990 campaign and his first years in Congress. "Bernie is a very demanding guy," says Fiermonte. "He has very high expectations, and he expects people to meet them. But he's a good boss. I wouldn't be with him otherwise."

Chris Graff covered Sanders for twenty-five years as Vermont's AP bureau chief. "Bernie has no social skills, no sense of humor, and he's quick to boil over," Graff says. "He's the most unpolitical person in politics I've ever come across."

Many of his colleagues in Congress would concur. He is known in the House and Senate as someone willing to express and stick to his positions but unable to compromise. "I admired him for his willingness to take stands for what he believed," says former congressman Barney Frank. "He went for the ideal, but he was not part of the legislative process. He chose to be an outsider."

He was seen as both an outsider and a true believer—in himself. "Bernie believes that he's right and that what he wants is for the greater good," says Susan Russ, Senator Jim Jeffords's longtime chief of staff. "He doesn't compromise. He picks friends and enemies. Once he decides you are one of them, he won't be helpful." Russ, now a political consultant in Houston, adds, "Most of us play by the rule that today's enemy could be tomorrow's friend. I don't think Bernie played that way. It was 'Play in my sandbox or get out.'"

Not many legislators fit in Sanders's sandbox. After sixteen years in the House and nine in the Senate, he has few friends in either body. Not one Vermont officeholder, congressman, or senator has endorsed him for president.

Which highlights Sanders's essential contradiction: he can reach crowds with soaring oratory but, as Judith Levine points out, he cannot connect with individuals. He has rarely seen a baby he wants to kiss, a hand he needs to shake, a back he'd like to slap. After whipping up crowds in New Hampshire, Wisconsin, and Iowa during a test run for his presidential campaign, he ignored pleas to stick around and mix with admirers. "Gotta go," he would mumble, then speed off to the next event.

If he has a sense of humor, it's on the dry side. After his early midwestern campaign tour he sent an email to Richard Sugarman: "Good news from Iowa—I'm only 48 points behind."

Black lives did matter when Sanders took his campaign to South Carolina, the pivotal primary state after Iowa and New Hampshire. Healthy crowds came to hear him talk about economic injustice, but few among them were black, and to win South Carolina, black votes are essential.

★ ★ ★

In Sanders's defense, the media covered him with much less zeal and attention than they showered on Trump and Clinton. Trump because of the outrageous comments that spewed from his mouth every time he opened it: he was always good copy. Clinton for a variety of reasons: she was ahead in the polls; she was under investigation by the FBI for using her private email carrier for official communication while she was secretary of state; and she was married to Bill Clinton, who was always good copy. Sanders had been criticizing the "corporate media" since the 1980s, and the campaign coverage bore him out.

Take, for example, Sanders's speech in Gaston Hall at Georgetown University on November 19, 2015. Gaston is a cathedral to lectures and learning in the north tower of Healy Hall, a nineteenth-century Gothic Revival structure on Georgetown's main campus. Its coffered ceilings rise some hundred feet and bear the coats of arms of sixty other Jesuit universities in existence at the time it was completed. Murals of saints and paintings of Athena adorn the stage and ceiling. Barack Obama, John Kerry, Bill Clinton, Bono, and Jon Stewart have spoken or performed at Gaston. Few if any received the welcome that greeted Sanders. Gaston's 700 seats were packed when he stepped up to the lectern that afternoon.

Chants of "Bernie! Bernie! Bernie!" filled the hall long before Sanders arrived, followed by "We Want Bernie!" "Feel the Bern!" greeted him when he took the stage. Such adoration used to stun Sanders, prompting him to marvel aloud at the exuberance of the crowd and thank everyone for coming to hear him. On this occasion he wasted no time. He had to deliver his speech, explain what he understood socialism to be, and detail his plans to defeat ISIS.

He invoked FDR and Martin Luther King Jr. to put his brand of socialism in perspective: "Against the ferocious opposition of the ruling class of his day, people he called 'economic royalists,' Roosevelt implemented a series of programs that put millions of people back to work, took them out of dire poverty, and restored their faith in government. He redefined the relationship of the federal government to the people of our nation. He combated cynicism, fear, and despair. He reinvigorated democracy. He transformed our country, and that is exactly what we have to do today."

"And by the way," he added, almost everything FDR had proposed, "almost every program, every idea he introduced, was called 'socialist.'"

Sanders spent the lion's share of his time explaining his approach to socialism and why socialism should not scare Americans. And he succeeded in that.

Then, fifty minutes into the address, he turned to foreign affairs and terrorism, and for anyone listening with a journalistic ear, he made news. He didn't say, "Hey, I'm about to make news!" That's too bad because most reporters there missed it or, at best, downplayed it. Instead he said, "I'm not running for president to pursue reckless adventures abroad, but to rebuild America's strength at home." No surprise there. "I will never hesitate to defend this nation, but I will never send our sons and daughters to war under false pretense or pretenses, about dubious battles with no end in sight." Again, not earth-shattering.

"To my mind," he continued, "it is clear that the United States must pursue policies to destroy the brutal and barbaric ISIS regime and to create conditions that prevent fanatical extremist ideologies from flourishing. But we cannot—and should not—do it alone." And here, for the first time, Sanders called for the creation of "a new organization like NATO to confront the security threats of the twenty-first century." He insisted that defeating ISIS must involve a focused effort of the NATO nations, Russia, and Arab League members. "While the United States and other Western nations have the strength of our militaries and our political systems, the fight against ISIS is a struggle for the soul of Islam, and countering violent extremism and destroying ISIS must be done primarily by Muslim nations—with the strong support of their global partners."

With that, Bernie Sanders, candidate for the US presidency,

proposed a military alliance that expanded the countries in NATO to include Russia and Arab nations. It was a novel, bold idea. It would take leadership and persistence. And Sanders has demonstrated both.

The news that afternoon and the next day buried Sanders's remarks on the history of American socialism and barely mentioned his new proposal for countering terrorism. The media fascination of the day? Donald Trump suggests a database to track Muslims, and Ben Carson compares the prospect of Syrian refugees to the threat of a "rabid dog."

★ ★ ★

Mike Pattavina, a soybean farmer in southeastern Iowa, kept putting up "Bernie!" signs on his property, but they kept disappearing. So he got on his tractor and plowed BERNIE in sixty-foot-high capital letters over a quarter-acre of his land.

"I was on my tractor one day and thought, 'Well, I'll just try this,'" he told ABC News. "It worked out pretty good." He'd already harvested his crop and had a half hour to spare, so he freewheeled the letters. "I just want people to see it, and maybe, hopefully, some people can see it from the air. Just to show support for Bernie."

Pattavina noted that his town of Clarinda was "ultraconservative" but that he was sold on Sanders. "I think he's for the working-class people," the sixty-eight-year-old farmer said.

Pattavina was not the only farmer who liked what Sanders had to say enough to support him in the election. Sanders had the Vermont farmers with him, but they were precious few. His appeal stretched far beyond Vermont and New England, however. Family farmers in every state were backing Sanders. But when Pattavina said Sanders was for "working-class people," he hit on what might propel the candidate beyond even his own expectations.

Sanders's connection to white, working-class voters is part of his "secret sauce," according to Kevin Kelley of *Seven Days*, who wrote in August 2015, "Underlying all of Sanders's electoral successes is his ability to win the support of white working-class voters. Sanders's friends, former campaign staff, and academic analysts who have watched him over the decades agree on the elements that comprise his political repertoire: charisma, authenticity, trustworthiness, and simplicity and consistency of message. Sanders wins respect among moderates and even some conservatives, these sources add, by abstaining from ideology and by taking a pragmatic, but always principled, approach to governing and legislating."

If Sanders could proselytize enough members of the working class, regardless of complexion or craft, so that they too had had "enough with billionaires taking all the money," his campaign would have exceeded all expectations. Even more so if college students had joined the fold.

Walking into Gaston Hall, Sanders had passed hundreds of students waiting in the rain to hear him speak. Now, toward the end of his speech, he paused. He was finished explaining his brand of socialism, describing his strategy for stopping terrorists. He looked out across the rows of students before him and gazed up at the balconies filled with young faces. He told them how encouraged and energized he was at seeing the faces of so many young people receptive to his point of view. "When I talk about a political revolution, I'm talking about bringing in the voices of millions of people who have given up on the political process. When that happens, anything is possible."

Sanders had given that refrain a thousand times, but before this crowd of eager, impressionable, idealistic young people, it seemed to reach a new plateau, a moment that could even pass for intimacy and introspection, even transcendence.

"It's not just about electing Bernie Sanders to be president," he continued. "It's much more than that. No president can bring about the changes we're talking about unless millions of people stand up and fight back."

The students stood and roared.

Sanders meant what he said. He would have to use social media and other means to bring millions more people to his cause. He would have to register voters willing to punch his ticket. The "secret sauce" of his ability to attract working-class voters would have to work better than ever. But to succeed in his mission—and it is a mission—he would need them not merely to vote for him but also to show up after he was elected.

That's a tall order. But it's part and parcel of what he wrote in *Outsider in the House*: "Here is the great catch-22 of American politics: as long as low-income people do not vote or participate politically, they will be scapegoated. But as long as both major parties continue to ignore the problems of low-income citizens, the poor will see politics as irrelevant and won't vote or join the political process."

There is much truth in that statement. It is especially true regarding Sanders's crusade to get to the White House. He believes the majority of people can succeed and prosper. They just have to believe in Bernie—and in themselves.

★ TWELVE ★

FLATBUSH BERNS

"The world has come around to see things
like he does, through the same lens."
—Phil Fiermonte, 2015

O nce or twice a week in the summer and fall of 2015, Paul
Sliker finds himself carrying a bunch of "Bernie for President" lawn signs and campaign leaflets past the house where
Sanders rented a room back in the early 1960s, while he was
attending Brooklyn College. Sliker is a volunteer for "Team
Bernie," a loose-knit group organizing Brooklyn for Sanders's
presidential campaign.

"It gives me chills to think about what a young, radical
Jewish Sanders would have thought had he had the opportunity to glimpse outside his window and look at me in the
future," Sliker says. "It's pretty amazing how far he's gotten. I
don't think he would have believed it."

Sanders in 1960 and Sliker in 2015 have much in common. Both are idealistic and want to change the world. They combine the impatience of youth with the certainty that they have a better way of running the country. The difference is that Sanders at twenty didn't have a candidate to believe in; he simply believed in revolutionary change. Sliker at twenty-seven believes in Sanders.

"There's a tremendous amount of interest in Bernie all over Brooklyn," says Sliker, who runs his own communications and marketing firm. His interest propelled him to join Team Bernie. "We're trying to educate folks out in the neighborhoods. Many people don't know who Bernie is. It's the essence of a grassroots campaign."

The Brooklyn today bears little resemblance to the borough of the 1950s, especially in the neighborhoods in and around Flatbush, where Sanders grew up. The apartment building he lived in as a child remains on the corner of East 26th Street and Kings Highway, but it is now home primarily to older Russian Jews. His alma mater, James Madison High School, down the street from the building, was largely Jewish with a few Italians and Irish kids; now the students are African American and Caribbean, reflecting the demographic changes in Madison Park and that part of Flatbush. In other parts of Brooklyn entire neighborhoods of brownstones and stately apartment buildings have been discovered by young white and black millennials. They are moving in, renovating the buildings, and pushing out longtime residents in the kind of gentrification that is remaking cities from Philadelphia to San Francisco.

On the night of the first Democratic presidential primary debate, young Sanders fans gathered in bars and homes from

Bedford-Stuyvesant to Ditmas, Crown Heights to Sheepshead Bay to watch and cheer on their candidate. Sara DeLaney
came to the Dram Shop in Park Slope with her husband,
Chuck, and daughter, Lily, to watch Sanders take on Clinton
and the other candidates. "Brooklyn has exploded," she says.
"There are cranes everywhere. There are a lot of people moving
here from Manhattan." Like the DeLaneys, others had shown
up at the Dram Shop for an event organized by the Sanders
camp. "I wanted to be with a group of people who are excited
by the issues Bernie is raising. I was rooting for him as soon as
he announced his candidacy."

Why Bernie Sanders?

"Because he believes in a living wage, and so do I," says
DeLaney. "No one can live on nine dollars an hour. And he's
right about the superwealthy controlling our political system.
An oligarchy is destructive. *Citizens United* is a travesty."

Says seventeen-year-old Lily, "It's un-American."

It's an odd demographic turn: the Brooklyn that immigrants once aspired to leave for Manhattan is now a destina-
tion for young entrepreneurs and professionals eager to exit
Manhattan. Of course there are lifers and Brooklyn natives
like Steve Slavin, and there are still rough neighborhoods like
Brownsville, but by and large Brooklyn is for Bernie.

Says Sliker, "It's a Bernie-fest on the Brooklyn College
campus."

★ ★ ★

When Sanders spent his freshman year at Brooklyn College,
the students were predominantly Jewish. That's not the case

in 2015. Flatbush has changed; the college has a multicultural campus. Religion matters less.

Perhaps that's why it doesn't seem to matter that Bernie Sanders is Jewish. When John F. Kennedy ran for president in 1960, the fact that he was Catholic was a major issue. Was the United States ready for its first Catholic president? Would that put the Pope and the Vatican in control of the government, many people wondered?

When Senator Joe Lieberman ran as the Democratic Party's nominee for vice president in 2000, the prospect that a Jew might occupy the Oval Office became a topic of conversation and concern. So why has Bernie Sanders's Jewish upbringing not entered the public debate? He would, after all, be the first Jewish president. How could that not matter?

It could be that Sanders has other, more outstanding distinctions. Maybe being a socialist of some sort obscures his religious affiliation. It could be that he wears his Jewishness so boldly and obviously, in the mannerisms and accent that Larry David so often lampoons, that voters have gotten used to it. Perhaps the fact that America has elected and re-elected an African American president inoculates a Jewish candidate.

Or it could be that the closer Sanders gets to winning the primary or the general election, the more his religion will become an issue.

Sanders doesn't broadcast the fact that he was raised a Jew. His wife, Jane, was raised a Catholic. She says they are both spiritual and adhere to basic Judeo-Christian beliefs. In August 2013 Senator Sanders, his brother and their wives traveled to Słopnice, Poland, the village that Eli Sanders left when he was 17 to come to America. Mayor Adam Soltys gave them a tour of the still small town. They visited the town's war memorials, local schools and the place where the ancestral family home once stood. According to an account in *Tablet*, the Sanders boys pressed the mayor for details about their family. He said Eli's half brother was a leader of Słopnice's Jewish community at the time the Nazis invaded Poland. "Which of course," Larry Sanders said, "meant he was one of the first to be killed."

That means the part of Bernie Sanders that connects him to Jews slaughtered in the Holocaust will not go away.

★ ★ ★

But why does Bernie Sanders matter?

Todd Gitlin, a professor of journalism and sociology at Columbia University and author of *The Sixties: Years of Hope, Days of Rage*, sees a Sanders moment culled from the counterculture. "It may have seemed, only a few years ago," Gitlin wrote in the *New York Times*, "that the '60s radical moment was consigned to documentaries on Woodstock, pushed out of the spotlight for Occupy Wall Street and a new generation of activists to enter stage left. But here it is again. And it is perfectly timed to crusade against what Senator Bernie Sanders of Vermont, who is seeking the Democratic presidential nomination, calls 'oligarchy.'"

That might explain how Sanders fits into Gitlin's conception of the progressive movement, but what makes Sanders matter to farmers in Iowa, fishermen in Oregon, construction workers in Nevada, retirees in Florida, schoolteachers in New Hampshire, and young executives in Brooklyn?

For starters, Sanders has tapped into the antipolitician

sentiment among American voters. Politicians from Reagan to Trump have successfully mined the antiestablishment vein that runs through the American electorate. It just so happens that Sanders's righteous rage is rooted in the reality of severe income inequality.

The irony of Sanders running against the political establishment is rich. He's been a professional politician since 1971, running for office every two years until he became a US senator and got a longer term. Somehow he obscures that part of his brand.

For the short term, at least through the 2016 campaign, Sanders will continue to have an impact on the candidates, the discussions, and the tenor of the debates. Months before the primary, he already had steered the conversation toward populist values. Hillary Clinton's strategists must worry about the sheer numbers that Sanders is wracking up, both in attendance at his events and in his poll numbers. They cannot afford to lose Sanders's progressive followers, either in the primary or general elections, so they must tack to the left. Sanders has introduced legislation to raise the minimum wage to $15 an hour, and he hits that note in virtually every speech. Clinton wants to raise it to $12. Sanders could well force her closer to $15. Both Sanders and Clinton have put forth plans to reform immigration laws, but Sanders goes much further and deeper in making the US more welcoming to newcomers. The *New York Times* applauded the senator's plan, compared it to Clinton's and concluded: "We hope she is inspired to match his boldness."

Bernie Sanders will matter far beyond the campaign season because his message has become painfully relevant. The gap between the wealthy and the rest of America is wider than at any time since 1928, according to a study by the Pew Research Center, and that gap is more obvious because of the ease and ubiquity of communications in the digital world.

When Sanders says too many American families are working two or more jobs just to remain in the middle class, Americans across the country nod their heads in agreement.

When he notes that most industrialized nations provide paid leave for parents of newborns and observes, "If that's not family values, I don't know what is," people applaud.

When he asks college students whether it makes sense that American students have to take out loans at exorbitant interest rates to pay for tuition they swivel their heads and say: "No." By constantly reminding voters that tuition to state universities should and could be free, Sanders is creating a movement where none existed. The same is true for health care reform. Sanders would go beyond the complex system set up by President Obama in the Affordable Care Act. Thanks to Sanders, a universal health care system, like Medicare for all Americans, is on the table.

Sanders hammers again and again on the fact that a few wealthy families donate the preponderance of funds to political campaigns. The Koch brothers, for instance, announced that they would contribute nearly $1 billion to elect candidates in 2016. A *New York Times* investigation proved Sanders right when it found that 158 families—mostly white and male-dominated—donate the lion's share to campaigns. "The average Joe now wants to talk about campaign finance reform," says Paul Sliker. "People hear what Sanders is saying about our political system and hear someone who will stand by what he says, because they know he isn't bought out by some billionaire or super PAC. He represents a crucial step in the right direction. He matters because he represents the possibility of a revival in American democracy."

Has a subject as arcane as money in politics ever incited such rage?

Sanders has been giving what his aides call "the oligarchy speech" for decades. As Phil Fiermonte says, "The world has come around to see things like he does, through the same lens."

★ ★ ★

That lens is showing Sliker and the volunteers at Team Bernie the way forward. "No one is out here to put another line on his or her résumé," he says. "We are united to get a candidate elected who makes some sense."

But while Sanders might make sense to the young white folks who have recently moved to Brooklyn, he's a harder sell to the people of color who live in and around Flatbush. "My best pitch is 'Vote for a presidential candidate who grew up down the street,'" Sliker says. "It stops people in their tracks. They don't know about Bernie Sanders. But they are starting to understand. Flatbush is warming to Bernie."

Gitlin writes that the secret of Sanders's appeal is that he delivers "a moralistic politics that takes seriously the democratic proposition that elected officials must deliver results." In other words, Sanders knows what are the right and just things to do, and he expects the government to help make those things happen.

Pundits and prognosticators peered into polls in late summer of 2015 and declared that Bernard Sanders had peaked.

Perhaps. But that doesn't mean that he would walk away from the campaign. His campaign showed all the signs of an appartus capable of laying siege to the campaign through the 2016 Democratic Convention in Philadelphia. The reason was money. Sanders railed against the campaign finance system that created super PACs—political action committees that could raise and spend unlimited amounts of cash. He disavowed them and raised funds from millions of people in small doses. By using the Internet and social media, Sanders was reaching people who would be receptive to his beliefs. He was salting away millions of dollars at a rate equal to Hillary Clinton's campaign, but hers was financed by bundlers, PACs and wealthy donors. What's more, Sanders is frugal to a fault and hoards contributions. That points to the very real possibility that he will have reserves stashed away to take his campaign far beyond 2016.

Ultimately, Bernie Sanders matters if he's successful in his lifelong mission of creating a movement of millions of people who will mount the "political revolution" he believes is necessary. He's been saying for decades that no one leader can bring about the kinds of changes he envisions, in health care and campaign finance and workers rights. In the campaign he repeated the same riff in his stump speeches. For Sanders it doesn't take a village; it takes a revolution.

It's complicated, of course, but Sanders is delivering what a great many Americans consider to be the truth, painful though it might be, and he's giving them hope and an opportunity to change the country's course: from exclusion to inclusion, from hoarding to sharing, from oligarchy back to democracy.

That's why he matters.

BIBLIOGRAPHY

Senator Bernard Sanders declined repeated requests to participate in this book. I was able to interview Jane O'Meara Sanders in the Burlington campaign headquarters for thirty minutes. The great majority of material for this book comes from original reporting in Brooklyn, Vermont, and Washington, DC. The sources and places are noted in each chapter.

I relied heavily on a number of newspaper and magazine articles and books.

MAGAZINE ARTICLES

In addition to the sources listed below, the Vermont weekly *Seven Days* constantly covered Sanders well over the years and during the presidential campaign.

Russell Banks, "Bernie Sanders, the Socialist Mayor," reprinted in *Atlantic*, October 5, 2015, http://www.theatlantic.com /politics/archive/2015/10/bernie-sanders-mayor/407413 / is a revealing profile written in the 1980s.

Louis Berney, "Sanders on Sanders: Meet the Mayor," *Vermont Vanguard*, March 13, 1981, https://www.scribd.com

/fullscreen/239115640?access_key=key-Qtyj21PgKz9
doOEzwHrA&allow_share=true&escape=false&view
_mode=scroll. Berney, my *Rutland Herald* colleague,
caught Sanders just as he was elected mayor in 1981.

Jas Chana, "Straight Outta Brooklyn by Way of Vermont: The
Bernie Sanders Story," *Tablet*, August 20, 2015, http://
www.tabletmag.com/jewish-news-and-politics/192931
/bernie-sanders-story.

Mark Jacobson, "Bernie Sanders for President? Why Not Try
a Real Socialist for a Change," *New York*, December 28,
2014, http://nymag.com/daily/intelligencer/2014/12/ber
nie-sanders-for-president-why-not.html#. Jacobson got
under Sanders's skin and into his brain in this terrific profile.

Michael Kruz, "Bernie Sanders Has a Secret," *Politico Magazine*, July 9, 2015, http://www.politico.com/magazine
/story/2015/07/bernie-sanders-vermont-119927_full
.html#.VlPJrGSrSjk. Kruz unearthed the best details of
Sanders's early days in Vermont.

Jill Lawrence, "Profiles in negotiation: the Veterans Deal of
2014," Center for Effective Public Management at Brookings, July 2, 2015, http://www.brookings.edu/research/pa
pers/2015/07/profiles-negotiation-veterans-lawrence.

Mark Leibovich, "The Socialist Senator," *New York Times Magazine*, January 21, 2007, http://www.nytimes.com/2007
/01/21/magazine/21Sanders.t.html?pagewanted=all&
_r=0. Leibovich's profile of Senator Sanders is stellar.

Paul Lewis, "Inside the Mind of Bernie Sanders: Unbowed,
Unchanged, and Unafraid of a Good Fight," *Rawstory*,
June 19, 2015, http://www.rawstory.com/2015/06/inside

-the-mind-of-bernie-sanders-unbowed-unchanged-and
-unafraid-of-a-good-fight/.

Tim Murphy, "How Bernie Sanders Learned to Be a Real Politician," *Mother Jones*, May 26, 2015, http://www .motherjones.com/politics/2015/05/young-bernie-sand ers-liberty-union-vermont. Murphy did the best overall reporting on Sanders, day after day.

Simon van Zuylen-Wood, "I'm Right and Everybody Else Is Wrong. Clear about That?," *National Journal*, June 18, 2014, http://www.nationaljournal.com/magazine/i-m-right-and -everybody-else-is-wrong-clear-about-that-20140618. This article captures Sanders as his most curmudgeonly self.

BOOKS

Greg Guma, *The People's Republic: Vermont and the Sanders Revolution* (New England Press, 1993).

Steven Rosenfeld, *Making History in Vermont: The Election of a Socialist to Congress* (Hollowbrook, 1992).

Jack Ross, *The Socialist Party of America: A Complete History* (University of Nebraska Press, 2015).

Mike Royko, *Boss: Richard Daley of Chicago* (Plume, 1988).

Bernie Sanders with Huck Gutman, *Outsider in the House* (Penguin, 1998).

Steven Soifer, *The Socialist Mayor: Bernard Sanders in Burling-ton, Vermont* (Praeger, 1991).

ACKNOWLEDGMENTS

Writing this book was a group project. I could not possibly have completed it in such a short amount of time without massive amounts of help. It took a small newsroom.

Four able students from the University of Maryland's Merrill School of Journalism volunteered their time and skills to research part of the Sanders story. Clarice Silber looked into his upbringing in Brooklyn and how it affected him. Joe Antoshak investigated the life-changing years Sanders spent at the University of Chicago. Fatimah Waseem, a recent graduate, delved into his sixteen years in the House of Representatives. Teresa Lo delivered a comprehensive report on Sanders's Senate years.

Thanks go to my publisher at *Washingtonian*, Cathy Merrill Williams, for paving my way into the journalism school, and to Adrianne Flynn for connecting me with the students.

Ken DeCell is the ideal editor. My editor for many years at *Washingtonian*, Ken polished my prose, made sense of my meanderings, and turned out cleaner copy in hours. It would have been a rough read without his touch. And it would have been much less accurate and full of misspelled names without Elizabeth Elving's fact-checking prowess.

Washingtonian editor Mike Shaeffer made a crucial connection to *Boston Magazine*, which sent me on the campaign trail to profile Sanders for its October 2015 issue. That piece benefited from Chris Vogel's encouragement and editing.

Tom Lindenfeld was my muse in politics, writing, and perspective.

I first covered Bernie Sanders in 1976, when I was reporting for the *Rutland Herald*. For this book I was lucky enough to reach back to former colleagues and competitors for guidance, especially AP's Chris Graff; Scott MacKay, who covered Sanders for the *Burlington Free Press*; Vermont Public Radio's John Dillon; and Bob Sherman, journalist, lobbyist, and farmer.

My best and deepest insights into Sanders came from his friends and associates: Jim Rader, John Franco, and Richard Sugarman. Greg Guma, author of *The People's Republic: Vermont and the Sanders Revolution*, was generous with his time and analysis. My dear friend Andy Snyder, with whom I started the Rutland Food Co-op in 1974, went on to serve in the Vermont Legislature and Department of Education, where he had opportunities to work with Sanders. His anecdotes and analysis always rang true. Thanks to Dexter Randall for welcoming me into his home and describing how Sanders became ingrained with Vermont farmers.

Genevieve and Rick Drutchas sheltered and fed me every time I showed up on their doorstep. And their honey was way better than mine.

In Brooklyn, Steve Slavin gave me the Sanders tour of

Madison Park and made me feel at home. Thanks to Lou Howort for inviting me in to talk about running track with Sanders. Myron Kalin made me laugh and shared his Madison High yearbook with Bernie Sanders's inscription.

The idea for this book came from conversations with my agent and friend, Howard Yoon. Publishers have little appetite for unauthorized biographies of current political figures. It took Lucas Wittmann at Regan Arts to understand the value of a Sanders biography and to entrust me with the project. He proved to be the ideal editor, encouraging without being too demanding for an impossibly tight deadline.

I was nourished by the unwavering love of my three far-flung daughters: Anna in Juba, Rose in Berlin, Claire in Washington, DC. Stella, our yellow lab, always liked me.

Here's to my lovely wife, Louise, who never doubted her Jewish writer friend.

ABOUT THE AUTHOR

Harry Jaffe, *Washingtonian*'s editor at large, is a leading journalist covering the city of Washington, DC—its politics, its crime, its heroes and villains. Beyond Washington, Jaffe's work has been published in Yahoo News, *Men's Health*, *Harper's*, *Esquire*, and newspapers from the *San Francisco Examiner* to the *Philadelphia Inquirer*. He's appeared in documentary films, and on television and radio across the country and throughout Europe.